What Others are Saying

Nancy Gaskins radiates a super-charged, high-energy presence that immediately involves people and has them responding to her exciting challenge to desire, create, and live the American Dream! With her quick wit, flair for drama and unique insight into human behavior, Nancy delivers solid content and practical techniques that can be put to use immediately at work and home. For those who dare to leave a mediocre live behind, & desire to be extraordinary, just follow her sage advice!

Seminar Attendees

Wow! Sometimes all we need is a little wake-up call to make us realize how much we are missing out in life! The "*Live Like You Are Dying*" Seminar rekindled my dreams, made me realize that it's never too late to get started, & gave me the inspiration to go home and get busy! Thank You, Nancy.

Military Spouse
Stuttgart, Germany

I attended my first AWAG conference this last fall. I signed up to take a class given by Nancy Gaskins. She inspired the whole class. She had us dancing, talking and laughing so hard that we were crying. During the class it was like a light bulb had went off. You always think about what if… and what to do to make things better. Then you meet Nancy and she tells you straight to the point and you get this feeling of yeah I can do that…better yet **I want to do that!** I left the class and I felt like I was walking on air…it just all made so much sense.

I remember my husband picking me up after the conference and we had a 30 minute drive home. He couldn't get a word in for I was talking about the great classes I had just taken and how it would be something that he should do for training time with his Soldiers! Thanks for all the inspiration!

V. Brantley, Military Spouse
Wuerzberg Germany

Americans Face Challenge-to-Succeed

I think the Challenge-to-Succeed Competition is not only a fantastic idea, but I think it will help to inspire entire communities much like the "Biggest Loser" competition did to lose weight. Take it on the road with the winners from each community inspiring others towards success!

Mary Markos, Military Spouse
Grafenwoehr, Germany

Dollar-a-Day Real Estate

Investment Strategies for Everyday People

In Pursuit of the American Dream

a Life Enrichment Book Series

#2

Nancy Gaskins, MBA

the Dollar-a-Day Real Estate Investor

www.iTrainInvestors.com

iUniverse, Inc.
New York Bloomington

Dollar a Day Real Estate
Investment Strategies for Everyday People

iUniverse books may be ordered through booksellers or by contacting:

iUniverse
1663 Liberty Drive
Bloomington, IN 47403
www.iuniverse.com
1-800-Authors (1-800-288-4677)

*Because of the dynamic nature of the Internet, any Web addresses or links contained in
this book may have changed since publication and may no longer be valid. The views
expressed in this work are solely those of the author and do not necessarily reflect the
views of the publisher, and the publisher hereby disclaims any responsibility for them.*

ISBN: 978-1-4502-3687-4 (sc)
ISBN: 978-1-4502-3688-1 (ebook)

Printed in the United States of America

iUniverse rev. date: 06/29/2010

Contents

PART VII

APPENDIX

PART VIII

Dear _____

Carpe Diem! (Seize the Day)
TODAY is the first day of the rest of your life!

Nancy G's Recipe for a Successful Day

Remember to live each day as if it's your last; with NO regrets.
May you always wake up happy and rested, with a smile on your
face, & go to bed content from your accomplishments for the day.

_____   _____

Date

This Special Edition is published
in Honor of our

American Military Families;

For without their daily self-less service and sacrifices
The American Dream would not be possible.

Dedication

For my brother,

Roger Quinn, Ag Pilot
Paragould, Arkansas

The best brother a gal could ever have.
Words could never express how much you mean to me.

Our daily chat sessions keep me motivated, and always laughing.
When I'm down in the dumps,
You're always right there…giving me a nice
"reality" check…*Roger Quinn style.*

You serve as a constant reminder
of how important it is to keep dreaming BIG,
to Never, EVER, give up on my dreams…

Our <u>Legacy</u> has just begun, brother!
I love you!

Dollar-a-Day Real Estate Investment Program

Investment Strategies for Everyday People

Course Objective:

Upon completion, the student will have learned how to use "*Dollar-a-Day Real Estate Investing*," as a viable strategy to invest in real estate, fund their own real estate investment company, and to create residual income… without all the hassles and headaches of buyers, sellers, and tenants.

What to Expect

The American Dream is alive and well! Imagine being part of an exciting life-changing organization full of individuals that want nothing more than for you to get absolutely everything you want out of life, & are totally 100% committed to helping you achieve all that…& more!

The Dollar-a-Day Real Estate Investment Program has been created to help *transform lives & improve communities world-wide* this year by providing an affordable option for everyday people to invest in real estate for less than the price of one soft drink per day. For an investment of only $1 per day, almost everyone you know will now be able to *participate and profit* from the current real estate and economic crises.

Earn as You Learn: Students have the opportunity to "earn as you learn," as they complete their OJT (on the job training) homework assignments.

100% Job Placement Guarantee

Upon successful completion, each student will be eligible to join the Dollar-a-Day Real Estate Investment Company team. This job placement offer expires 90-days from date of course completion.

Support

Nancy is available to answer any questions or concerns by email on a daily basis. You may also participate in discussions sessions on-line.
Email Nancy.Gaskins@operationHSH.com, be sure to include the words, "Student ?" in the subject line.

Each **Thursday**, and the *last week of each month* is reserved for 1-on-1 and group coaching sessions with Nancy. Each month, we will work together to establish personal and professional goals. These sessions are available on-line, or by telephone.

Course Requirements:

Microsoft Office Applications and Internet access is a requirement. Chat capability must be enabled if you wish to participate in chat discussions. Homework assignments and/or Exams are due electronically *no later than Mondays, 6pm* of the week following the assignment.

Week by Week

Enrollment is available on a four week rotating calendar month cycle, and all coursework is expected to be completed within 60 days of enrollment. You may request an extension for an additional 30-days. Each week of the month is numbered and will be focused on the following:

Week 1: Dollar-a-Day Real Estate Investment Program Overview

This session provides a complete overview of the Dollar a Day Real Estate Investment Company, including the background, vision, mission, and objectives for the upcoming year. The Dollar a Day Real Estate Investment Training Program is introduced, including the "Earn as You Learn" on the job training component.

Week 2: Create Your Financial Objectives

The second week of each month is focused on creating and revising your financial objectives for the upcoming month, next 90-days, and upcoming year. On-line discussions and competitions will be available continuously to help inspire students to continuously enlarge their visions, provide camaraderie, and allow a healthy dose of competition among peers.

Week 3: Earn as You Learn; Building Your Team

This week is for implementing your strategic plan; i.e. building your business and growing your financial net worth *exponentially* through networking and teambuilding efforts.

Week 4: Coaching Sessions with Nancy

Each Thursday, and the last week of each month is reserved for 1-on-1 and group coaching sessions with Nancy. Each month, we will work together to establish personal and professional goals. These sessions are available on-line, or by telephone.

Executive Summary

Challenge to Succeed 2010

1. Overview
2. Mission and Vision
3. Client Services
4. How to Start & Grow a Network
5. Show Me the Money
6. How do I Join?
7. Upcoming Investment Cycle

Take a few minutes to read this Executive Summary to get a quick overview, and to learn how becoming a Dollar-a-Day Real Estate Investor can benefit you and your family this year. Read the rest of the book for a more in depth look at the options available for you as a Dollar-a-Day Real Estate Investor. Afterwards, I invite you to visit my website, www.iTrainInvestors.com, to accept my personal invitation to join the Dollar-a-Day Real Estate Investor Network

To Your Financial Success!

Nancy S. Gaskins, MBA
the Dollar-a-Day Real Estate Investor

Point to Ponder:
Opportunity is never lost; if you don't find it, someone else will. ~Unknown

Challenge to Succeed 2010

Transforming America, ONE Family at a Time

I am no politician or expert in economics, but I have come up with my own 5 Point Plan for creating REAL change in America this year. You may be surprised to learn that none of them have anything to do with the current recession, unemployment rate, politics, or the Obama administration.

There is no need to wait for the recession to end to experience change in America or anywhere world-wide. Change can begin immediately and results could be visible within as short of time as 30-days! I encourage you to challenge your family members, neighbors, co-workers, bosses, competitors, and communities to accept the Challenge 2 Succeed 2010 and make the commitment to help transform America one person, family, business, and community at a time.

Imagine the following: People would not be stuck in dead end jobs that they hated, relationships and marriages would flourish, finances would improve, stress levels would go down, our health would improve, businesses would grow at all time record highs, our communities would be revitalized, our government agencies would be held accountable for results, our economy would thrive, and our great nation would finally experience the real change that she so desperately needs; "a new awakening and revival of the long forgotten healthy pursuit of the American Dream." Do you remember that dream?

The idea of the American Dream was that each one of us has the chance to achieve success and prosperity. That concept did not include any mention that we are entitled to the dream just by breathing air or taking up space. If the American Constitution gives us the right to life, liberty, & the pursuit of happiness, just where does our personal responsibility begin and end?

Creating real change in America this year will have to begin on a personal level with each one of us, beginning at home, in our neighborhoods, businesses, and communities.

5 Cornerstones Required to Transform America

#1. Real change will begin when each and every American accepts full responsibility for their own life. We should immediately stop blaming our President, government, economy, community, bosses, co-workers, competitors, and family members for our bad luck and expect them to change our present circumstances or give us the winning lottery ticket to life.

#2. Accept the fact that you are where you are in life today, because of the choices that you made yesterday and the day before. If you don't like where you are today, quit doing what you did yesterday and the day before. Learn from your past mistakes and quit repeating them!

#3. Decide exactly what it is that you want out of your life, and create a detailed strategic plan to help you get from where you are to where you want to be in life. Most people fail miserably because they have never taken the time to really decide what they want. People tend to focus on what they don't want, and spend more time planning their weddings or vacations than they do on their life. If you don't have a plan for your life, your life will be left to chance. Are you willing to take that gamble?

Based on the increasing numbers of casino establishments being built and bankrolled, the number of gambling addiction problems being reported, and the effects of the instant lottery craze on the lives of so many Americans, it appears that we have already chosen to gamble with our lives and leave our fates left to chance. I believe there is a much safer, more effective, reliable route to achieve the same results: how about creating a fool-proof well thought out plan that doesn't include chance? Sound too hard and complicated? Think again.

#4. Surround yourself with people who can help you achieve your goals. Do not reinvent the wheel; network, ask questions, seek advice, share information and resources with others. If you want to soar with the eagles, quit spending time with the turkeys! Who are you hanging out with? Perhaps you have not reached the level of success in life that you desire because of the people with whom you associate. Who gives you advice? Are they living a life of mediocrity or living the American Dream? It has been proven that your income and lifestyle is a direct reflection and average of the people that you hang out with on a regular basis. Think about that statement long and hard.

#5. Keep score, make course corrections as necessary, and never give up! Most people quit after just one failure. This is a mistake. How do you know whether you have "arrived" if you have not made your destination clear? How far ahead or behind have you become? What is your benchmark?

These 5 cornerstones may seem a bit simplistic at first glance, but don't be deceived. Once you internalize and fully commit to implementing these principles 100% in all areas of your life; i.e. your personal life, your business, your career, your church, your community efforts...I guarantee that you will experience a radical transformation like none before.

Just how much better off would Americans, neighborhoods, communities, businesses, America, and the world would be if we would just take some time this year to focus on improving our own lives and communities in which we live? I predict that the results will be staggering.

Email me if you would like to join me in my commitment to accept the *"Challenge to Succeed"* this year in an effort to help transform America, one family at a time!

1. Overview

To the best of my recollection, I have moved twenty-four times throughout my twenty-six years of marriage. The majority of that time I was a military spouse paying RENT to landlords all over the world. Since I have lived coast to coast, and world-wide, the amount of rent that I have paid has varied throughout the years, but one fact remains constant…my monthly rent checks put thousands upon thousands of dollars into some real estate investor's bank account!

Should You Buy or Rent?

I used to cringe every month when I paid rent, and would constantly dream of that special day when I would finally have a home to call my very own. Sometimes renting makes financial sense, sometimes it doesn't. For people constantly on the move, like me, once you crunch the numbers, most of the time it doesn't really make "financial" sense to purchase a home. For those that decide to purchase, it usually is an *emotional* decision, and not a sound financial business decision.

Robert Kiyosaki, author of the Rich Dad, Poor Dad financial book series, shocked everyone when he began teaching that a home mortgage is actually a "liability" and not an asset. He differentiates the two by explaining if something puts money IN your pocket, it's an asset; if it takes money OUT, or cost you money, it should be considered a liability. This is contrary to what most people have been taught and conditioned to believe throughout the years. The only way to properly convert a mortgage into an ASSET, is to make sure that the rental income generated is sufficient to cover all expenses, <u>and</u> provides you with additional cash flow each and every month.

How to Build Wealth

To build wealth, which in financial terms is called *Net Worth*, your assets must be greater than your liabilities. In other words, what you "own," must be greater than what you "owe." In a business, *Net Income* is calculated by subtracting the operating expenses from the revenue generated for the month. The goal of course, is to achieve profitability; i.e. to have more income than expenses. Although these two terms are very important to your overall financial well-being, understanding *Cash Flow* (cash IN, cash OUT) should probably be your first priority because lack of adequate "cash flow" is the number one reason cited for financial failure for both individuals as well as businesses.

Real Estate: the Ultimate Investment?

How many times have you wrote out a check to pay rent and wished that YOU were the one "depositing" rent checks, instead of the one paying the rent? Have you ever driven by a housing subdivision, and dreamed about what it would be like to own a few of those properties, and wondered how you could do it? Do you know of anyone, or have you ever read about how it is possible for people to become wealthy by investing in real estate? Do you think it's possible?

I'm sure you have heard the saying that, "hindsight is twenty-twenty." If I could go back, knowing what I know now, one of my top priorities would be to do whatever it took to become a real estate investor from day one. I'm not saying that I would have never been a renter per se; I am saying that I would have been investing in real estate all along, and would now been able to enjoy and reap the rewards of having over 26 years of equity built up from paying down the mortgage using OPM (other people's money), property appreciation, and tax benefits!

Although I can't turn back the hands of time, the good news is that real estate investing is one of the best vehicles to use to make up for lost time, financially speaking. If you are arriving "late" in the financial ballgame, you still have time to recover, and become wealthy. Real Estate is one of the best financial tools available to help people achieve wealth due to a couple of major factors. Unlike other investments such as stocks and bonds, you don't have to pay for it in *full* at the time of purchase. You can pay little to no down payment, leverage and borrow money to pay for the remainder, and use the rental income generated to pay off the note. Over time, your equity will increase as you pay down your debt, and historically over the long run, real estate property tends to appreciate. Uncle Sam even offers tax benefits for those that invest in real estate for both personal and business purposes.

Wealth Building Strategies for Everyday People

Invest in Real Estate without all the hassles & headaches of buyers, sellers, and tenants! Have you ever dreamed of becoming a real estate investor, but have NO cash, credit, knowledge, experience, or time? Becoming a Real Estate Investor has never been easier or more affordable than now. For less than the price of one soft drink per day, becoming a Dollar a Day Real Estate Investor can help you turn your financial dreams into a reality this year!

Dollar-a-Day Real Estate Investments is a step-by-step, earn while you learn program created specifically to help everyday people profit from real estate based on their unique financial objectives and budget constraints. No credit, income, real estate knowledge, experience, or license is required.

Each of the Dollar-a-Day Real Estate Investment Program strategies was created specifically to provide Investors with one or more of the following financial benefits:

- Quick cash

- Fixed rates of return

- Residual income.

Now Accepting NEW Clients!

Welcome to the Dollar-a-Day Real Estate Investor Network! Dollar a Day Real Estate Investing gives everyday people an affordable, convenient option to invest in real estate for less than the price of one soft drink per day...*only $1 per day, $30 per month.*

Earn-While-You-Learn Option

In addition to having the affordable option to invest in real estate without the hassles and headaches of buyers, sellers, and tenants, Dollar a Day Real Estate Investing <u>also</u> provides a legitimate way to work from home, earn a living, build a retirement, and be able to spend more quality time doing the things you want, with the ones you love. For those that have no desire to become real estate investors, but would like to find a legitimate way to earn cash fast, make sure you read the Chapter titled, *"Affiliates."*

By Referral Only

New Client membership drives are now being scheduled in select cities across the nation. Invitations are *by referral only,* and will expire 10 days from the

United States Postal Service postmark date marked on your invitation, or on the date the Membership Drive has officially been completed in your city, or state. Feel free to email me at Nancy.Gaskins@operationHSH.com if you have any questions or to schedule a Membership Drive in your community!

Company Overview

The Dollar-a-Day Real Estate Investment Company is a private real estate investment and training company. The primary strategy that will be taught and used by Dollar-a-Day Real Estate Investors is to buy residential real estate and vacation rental properties at a discount, with cold-hard <u>CASH</u>.

I then fix them up and rent or sell to private individuals. I finance these deals with private funds from Investors in my Private Investor Network that are looking for the (a) high returns, (b) positive cash flow, or (c) residual income that real estate investing brings, as well as proceeds from the sale of Dollar-a-Day Real Estate training products and services.

I will teach you how to use Dollar-a-Day Real Estate Investing as a wealth-building strategy to (a) earn a fixed rate of return, (b) finance your very own real estate investment portfolio from the ground up, …starting with nothing, and (c) as a way to create and build a stream of residual income.

Investment Goals

My investment goal for the Network is to purchase a minimum of 10 to 12 residential and vacation properties per year, specializing first in purchasing properties within close proximity to top military installations, then moving to territories that our Client Chapters have researched, and found feasible to invest based on the Dollar-a-Day Real Estate Investment profile criteria.

I offer a convenient, affordable option for everyday people to invest in real estate for only $1 per day, $30 a month, hence the name, "*Dollar-a-Day Real Estate Investments.*" No restrictions, such as income or credit scores apply to participate. If you can afford $1 per day, $30 per month, you can become a Dollar-a-Day Real Estate Investor this year.

Private Financing Options

Once we have a sufficient number of Clients enrolled, Chapters in place, and are adequately funded, the goal will be to offer private financing options to Chapters who have completed the prerequisite training modules.

Clients are able to invest in real estate without all the hassles & headaches of buyers, sellers, and tenants. Clients receive a promissory note, and earn a fixed rate of return on their investment loans that is comparable to the 30-year mortgage rates offered in the United States. Since this is a <u>private</u> network, all Clients must be sponsored (referred) for eligibility.

Purpose

My name is <u>Nancy Gaskins</u>, and I created the Dollar-a-Day Real Estate Investor Network with the vision to give as many people as possible, including myself, an affordable option to take advantage of the real estate investment opportunities that are available in the marketplace today.

It's no secret that there are plenty of great deals from which to choose, and there are plenty of people that would also love the opportunity to become real estate investors so they could take advantage of all these great deals. The problem for the majority of people is they have no quick access to <u>cold-hard cash</u> or financial resources to finance these deals. Typically, only people with "deep pockets," can afford to take advantage of the opportunities available, *until now*. The Dollar-a-Day Real Estate Investor Network provides an affordable, cost-effective solution for *everyday people* to learn how to invest in real estate, for the small investment of only $1 per day.

TEAM – Together Everyone Achieves More

Working together as a "team," Dollar-a-Day Real Estate Investor trainees will learn how to identify, select, make offers, raise investment capital, purchase, and manage real estate investment properties in select communities throughout the United States. As part of your training, you will learn how to build a network and finance your real estate acquisitions.

Affordability

I am able to provide this service for Clients at the affordable price of only $1 per day, $30 per month, because of three primary reasons:

1. Dollar-a-Day Real Estate Investing has the potential for mass participation, and business success will be based on building strong, positive relationships with all Clients through team-based management techniques. I will encourage and facilitate "working" relationships among those in my Client Network because it will be mutually beneficial for everyone involved.

2. Satisfied Clients, will in turn, help build the company through word-of mouth advertising and referrals, and I will show my gratitude by paying Referral Fees as compensation for these efforts. Referral fees can be used for any purpose, individually,

or collectively as a group. I do encourage you to consider using at least a portion of your earnings to purchase real estate investment properties in your community as a way to help secure your financial future, as well as those in your network.

3. Having a large client base will allow access to large sums of capital to purchase more investment properties, which means the opportunity to earn more investment income for Clients. A large client base will also enable me to spread the cost of Management and Administration of the Network among many people, rather than just a few, which means a much lower cost to participate, which means more people can afford to become Dollar-a-Day Real Estate Investors.

Client Options

The Dollar-a-Day Real Estate Investor Network offers 4 different levels of service for Clients.

1. Associate
2. Investor: Levels I, II, & III
3. Affiliates
4. Sponsorships & Corporate Contributors

To learn the specifics and benefits of each option, read section 3 in this Executive Summary titled: *"Client Services."*

2. Mission and Vision

Mission

To inspire, educate, and motivate people to desire, create, and live a well-balanced life filled with purpose, achievement, and financial prosperity.

Vision

My vision is to build the largest, most profitable, private real estate investor network in the nation! The primary emphasis will be to structure the company, and provide products and services in such as way that will enable me to help every Client establish and achieve their personal financial goals each year.

I will request input from Clients on a continuous basis to help determine what products, services, and opportunities each of you would like to see made available through the Network. Together, we will build a company that we can all become proud with whom to be associated.

Pursue, Create, & Live the American Dream

I envision the Dollar-a-Day Real Estate Investor Network as not just merely a place to "park" your money to earn a fixed rate of return on real estate investments, but a *"golden"* opportunity for people to meet, network, build friendships, socialize, learn, ask questions, give and receive advice, discuss topics of interest, participate in upcoming investment opportunities and events, and to work together as a team to make enough money to finance the life of their dreams!

The bottom line is that my dream is for each of my Clients is to clearly define their dreams on a personal level, and actively pursue and live their "American Dream," through Dollar-a-Day Real Estate Investing.

Bonus Chapters – In Pursuit of the American Dream

I feel so strongly about my vision and mission statement that my book series is titled, "In Pursuit of the American Dream." Part I includes bonus material for you to learn more about "money," and the "American Dream."

3. Client Services

I offer 4 different levels of service for Clients in the Dollar-a-Day Real Estate Investor Network. Working together with each Client, and/or Chapter group, we will establish goals for the upcoming year, and come to an agreement on how best I can serve as your advisor, mentor, coach, and accountability partner.

1. Associates
2. Investor: Levels I, II, & III
3. Affiliates
4. Sponsorships & Corporate Contributors

1. Associates

An Associate is the Basic Client Membership. Investor trainees will receive individual and group coaching and mentoring sessions with Nancy Gaskins, access online Community discussion forums, training opportunities, and will have the option to participate in local, regional, and national Chapter Network activities as the client base expands and is able to support such activities.

Local Support

To be cost effective, and reach our investment targets, it will be necessary to have a large client base. To facilitate learning, provide accountability, local support, quick dissemination of information, and local investment opportunities, I will use of the same system that clubs and organizations use; local, district, regional, and national Dollar-a-Day Real Estate Investor Network Client Chapters.

Working together as a "team," Dollar-a-Day Real Estate Investor trainees will learn how to identify, select, make offers, raise investment capital, purchase, and manage real estate investment properties in select communities throughout the United States.

Associate Membership: $35 per year, plus
Tuition: $1 per day, $30 per month

2. Investors - Fixed Rates of Return

These Clients are interested in investing in real estate without all the hassles and headaches of buyers, sellers, and tenants. Investor Clients invest a minimum if $1 per day, $30 per month and prefer to earn a fixed rate of return on their investments. Clients in this category serve as our "lenders," their investments are structured as "loans," and rental income generated from each property is used to pay back each loan, plus the agreed upon fixed rate of interest. Investor Clients do not actively participate in real estate investment training activities.

Investor Membership: $35 per year, plus...
Level I$ 30 per month OR
Level II$ 50 per month OR
Level III$100 per month

3. Affiliates - Earn Cash Fast

These Members are interested in a legitimate way to work from home, earn a living, build a retirement, & be able to spend more quality of time doing the things they want with the ones they love. These people have big dreams and are looking for a way to finance them all...yesterday!

Affiliates are independent contractors that earn compensation by promoting our Company, Network, and products and services to others, online or offline, depending on their personal preferences. They serve as our Referral Partners. My Network is private, and I operate strictly from Referrals. Every time I gain a new client, or sell a product or service, the Sponsor gets paid a referral commission. Shouldn't that be you?

Team Builders
If you have a knack for teambuilding, love people, and would enjoy the

opportunity to get paid *extremely well* for helping people world-wide achieve their financial dreams, you should consider becoming an Affiliate. I provide the support system so you can focus on generating wealth for you and your team!

No Competition

Timing is everything, and sometimes it truly <u>does</u> pay to be first. This is definitely one of those times. Help me establish Dollar-a-Day Real Estate Real Estate Investor Client Chapters in communities across America and around the world, and I will help you achieve your financial dreams this year!

Dollar-a-Day Real Estate Investor Chapter territories are now available world-wide. I have not found any competition in the marketplace offering the same opportunities as Dollar-a-Day Real Estate Investments at this time. Commissions are paid daily, and bonuses are available both monthly and quarterly based on team performance.

Affiliates:

Associate Membership: $35 per year plus
Management Fee: $1 per day, $30 per month

To learn more, read the Chapters titled, "Affiliates," and "How to Build a Network."

4. Sponsors / Corporate Contributors

If you are an individual or business that offers a product or service that complements real estate investing, i.e. would be of benefit to Clients in my Network, you can join as a Sponsor or Corporate Contributor.

You have options to advertise on our website, in the Directory section of our books, monthly newsletters, and in training materials for workshops, seminars, and conferences.

A detailed listing in the on-line Membership Directory is included for FREE with your membership. You have affordable options to advertise in the Directory in the back of our book, which will soon be available to over 150,000 retailers online such as Barnes and Noble, www.bn.com, Amazon, www.amazon.com, and Books a Million to name just a few. Email for the latest opportunities and advertising rates.

Local Chapters

In the next section, I will cover the benefits of and ideas on how to start and grow a Dollar-a-Day Real Estate Investor Network Chapter in your community.

4. How to Start & Grow a Network

Imagine the excitement and money to be made when people realize they can become real estate investors for less than the price of one soft drink each day...$1 per day, $30 per month! There is no fine print, no credit, income, experience, or license required to participate. In fact you can even use Dollar-a-Day Real Estate Investment Company as a way to earn money while you are learning and investing!

Unlike stocks, bonds, and mutual funds, investing in real estate is *different*. You can literally see, touch and feel, and finance real estate purchases. You can drive by and "see" your money hard at work in your very own community, as well as communities across the nation!

Chapters Now Forming = Opportunity Knocking

My goal is to build a strong support network to help Clients learn from one another, stay motivated, focused, accountable, and on top of their game, so that they can achieve their financial and personal goals each year. My job is to ensure every Client is successful, and success will begin with you learning about the real estate investment opportunities located in your own community.

To provide this level of service to a large group, and remain cost effective at the same time, it will be necessary to establish Dollar-a-Day Real Estate Real Estate Investor Client Chapters in communities across America and around the world, at the local, district, region, and national levels.

Earn Cash Fast – Conduct a Membership Drive in Your Community

As a Dollar-a-Day Real Estate Investor, you have the option to earn some serious cash for yourself and/or your local Chapter by helping to establish local Chapters in your community. If you are looking for a way to earn some *seed money* to start or finance your own local real estate investment company, you should consider conducting a Dollar-a-Day Real Estate Investment Network Chapter Membership Drive in your community.

How does it work?

Membership Drives will be conducted once a year in select communities across the nation for the purpose of adding new Clients and new Chapters to the network. Each drive will last approximately 10-14 days, and each Chapter team will consist of a minimum of 25 people. Cash commissions will be paid for every new Membership that is attained during the Membership Drive, as well as from all referrals received from each new Member during the course of the first 30 days of membership.

Staying Focused

Dollar-a-Day Real Estate Investors should stay focused and spend the majority of their time on learning, investing, and mentoring others, which is why Client Membership drives will only be scheduled and held *once a year,* for a limited number of days in select communities across the nation.

How to Increase Your Odds for Success

I have dedicated many years to, and continue to educate myself on the principles for success, study the lives of successful people and companies, and stay abreast on how people are achieving financial independence through entrepreneurship and leadership development. Four common themes occur over and over again as ways to increase odds for financial success:

1. Own & operate your own business: It's next to impossible to become rich when you are trading your hours for wages.

2. A large percentage of people become millionaires by investing in real estate.

3. Surround yourself with people that are like-minded, know more than you do, and have a vested interest in your success.

4. It's not <u>what</u> you know, it's <u>who</u> you know that will determine your success of failure. Build a strong diverse network, and commit to helping one another succeed.

Here's the Deal

I have kept these 4 themes in mind when creating the Dollar-a-Day Real Estate Investor Network.

Each Chapter will have 5 individuals assigned to a team, including a Team Leader. There is a minimum goal of 25 people per Chapter, 5 Chapters per district, and 5 Districts in a Region. This type of system ensures that no one is left out, everyone has a voice that can be heard, everyone has a support team, everyone can easily be held accountable for results, and every single Client has a much better chance for success in reaching their goals!

Building Your Home Team

Despite what most people think, real estate investing is not an individual sport. To succeed as a real estate investor, you must build a <u>team</u> of qualified people that have a vested interest, and are as committed to your success as you are. Having this "home" team advantage can easily take years off your learning curve, help prevent you from making costly mistakes, and put more money in your pocket at the end of the day.

Each Chapter will identify, interview, and include the following professionals to their team: plumber, electrician, handyman, home inspector, property appraiser, licensed real estate agent specializing in your niche market, home staging consultant, insurance agent, real estate attorney, and a tax accountant that specializes in real estate investments. Depending on the investment goals of your Chapter, you might also want to include a licensed contractor, Management Company, cleaning service, landscaping/lawn care, and a mortgage broker.

In addition to earning the business of the Investors in your Chapter, the Dollar-a-Day Real Estate Investor Network teams of professionals will have the opportunity to advertise their services, showcase, and share their expertise in our Monthly Newsletters, participate in our Discussion Forums, and Network Events.

Dollar a Day Real Estate Investments...a very <u>exciting</u> deal!

Becoming a Dollar-a-Day Real Estate Investor will be your first and most important "deal." As one of my valued Clients, you will have access to my

Client "*Network...*" a place where people can come together to learn all about
"deals."

How to <u>look</u> for deals, where to go, who to know to <u>find</u> the deals, who to ask to make sure it's a <u>good</u> deal, <u>participate</u> in deals, request financial backing or learn how to structure a <u>great</u> deal, get a referral to an affordable contractor to help out with an <u>upcoming</u> deal, a place to find a top notch licensed real estate agent to handle <u>all</u> your deals!

Invitation to Join

The Dollar-a-Day Real Estate Investor Network makes it easy and affordable for <u>everyday people</u> to take advantage of all the real estate investment opportunity available in the marketplace today.

<u>Bottom line</u>...If you can afford $1 per day, $30 per month, you can become a real estate investor this year!

How to Join

Visit the Network website, www.iTrainInvestors.com, click on the Membership tab, and fill in the blanks..it's just that easy!

As you can see, for only $1 per day, the Dollar-a-Day Real Estate Investor Network has the potential to become a really, really, BIG deal!

Join Today......Isn't it time YOU become a "BIG Deal?"

Population Stats

There are currently 306 million people in the US, and 105 million households in America. Dollar-a-Day Real Estate Investing is not restricted to just the United States of America. That increases our market size potential to **6.7 billion** people in the world!

Benefits of a Large Client Base

One of the primary benefits of having a large client base is that we can offer a variety of top quality products and services at a fraction of the cost because we are able to purchase in bulk and pass the savings along to our clients.

Quick Access to Resources

Another benefit of a large client base is that we will have the capability to quickly tap into the knowledge base and experience of a large group of people world-wide to gain insight, seek advice, request help, and to supply encouragement in times of need 24 hours a day, 7 days a week.

Benefits of Local Chapters

I strongly encourage Clients to participate in Chapter activities and events not only for the learning and accountability aspect, but for the camraderie, support, and encouragement that is gained as a benefit of belonging to a diverse group that have similar goals and aspirations.

Committed to Your Success

It may come as a shock to you, but believe it or not, everyone in your life is not equipped or committed to help you succeed, nor does everyone in your life necessarily want you to succeed. Many times our closest friends, associates, and family members are toxic, have become our worst enemies, and will prevent you from achieving success in life. One of the most important benefits of having a local Chapter is for the support, encouragement, and accountability it will provide, which is vital for your success.

As a Client Member in the Dollar-a-Day Real Estate Investor Network, one of your primary responsibilities will be to encourage and help one another succeed. One of my favorite quotes is from master motivator Zig Ziglar, and I am committed to this philosophy. *"You can have anything in life that you want, as long as you help enough other people get what they want."*

What's Your Dream?

Would you like to double, triple, or quadruple your income this year? What's your dream? How about a new car, an all-expense paid vacation for your family, to become debt-free, build your dream home, quit your day job, spend more time with your loved ones, or retire? No matter what your financial goal is, you can easily achieve it this year by becoming a Client, and joining the Dollar-a-Day Real Estate Investor Network.

Accountability = Results
People don't plan to fail, they simply fail to plan! As a Client, I will teach you how to use my Life Management Goals system to help you to achieve any goal you may have for your life, no matter how small or grand it may be.

It's not a difficult process, but it does take a small time commitment for your success. Each month you will be asked to submit your goals for the month, along with your weekly plan of action. You will be assigned to an Accountability group that will help you stay focused, and on track. Results will be monitored and recognized at the individual, team, chapter, and company wide level.

Competition Pays

Who do you know that would enjoy the opportunity to increase their income this year? This is one of the few, rare business models where competition PAYS. The more Clients that we have promoting the Network, the higher the visibility, the more likely that people will join our network, and purchase one or more of our products and services. The larger our Network becomes, the more money we will have available to invest in real estate, and promote our Network. The more properties that we purchase, the more money we all make as investors…a true win-win for all of us!

Building a Membership Base

Contact me to schedule a Membership Drive for your community. Use the Membership Drive worksheets to create your personalized 90-day action plan. To help with recruiting efforts, official Membership Drives will be conducted a minimum of only one time per year. The rest of the year should be focused on learning, investing, and making money!

I will provide you with financial goal worksheets as a tool to help get your people excited enough to help you reach your Membership goals each year. By helping your members reach their personal financial goals each year, you can achieve your financial goals! You are free to recruit Members world-wide, but

I encourage people to get actively involved in a local Chapter. Everyone wins when we have more people affiliated with our company.

Promotional Strategies

You can pick and choose which strategies that works best for you; it might be something as simple as a magnetic sign for your car door, mailing out postcard invitations, handing out a referral card, posting referral cards on community billboards, placing a classified ad in a newspaper, or tweeting online! The strategies you can use and have at your disposal are only limited by your imagination!

Keep in mind that people are all different, and the more opportunities they have to be exposed to our message and invitation, the more likely they will be to join your group! I would strongly encourage you to build a team of referral partners and make sure that you have each of the promotional opportunities active in your community during your Membership Drive.

NO Selling is Required

We operate strictly from referrals, which mean that any sale that is generated must contain a referral source. Each time we gain business from anyone worldwide, the referral source will be paid a referral fee.

Although it does take a "sale," of a Client Membership, product, or service to earn a commission, to make it easy to build and grow Chapters locally, I have established a few ground rules for Membership and come up with a variety of strategies to use that will help to make this process almost effortless.

Membership Qualifications

To qualify and maintain membership eligibility in our Network, everyone must refer and Sponsor at least 3 people within the first 30-days of enrollment. As an incentive, a $10 Referral Fee will be paid for each referral. In essence, the new member can have his or her membership for *free* simply by referring more than 3 people within the first 30-days of enrollment!

Imagine This…

Imagine every Retail parking lot across America having one or more cars parked with our company logo on their car doors. Imagine everywhere you go seeing these very same signs. What about driving up and down the interstate highways seeing the same sign on cars as well as semi-truck doors?

Then you go home and find a Direct Mail Postcard Invitation in your mailbox. You go to the Beauty Shop and your stylist or nail tech asks you if you have heard about this company that teaches people how to invest in real estate for only one dollar a day. You open up the local classifieds newspaper, log on to E-bay, and low and behold there's the same company over and over again!

Do you think that would get some attention? Do you think that people would start to talk and inquire as to what that company is all about?

Retailers: If you are currently employed in the Retail industry, you have a competitive advantage in that you have a captive audience at your disposal on a daily basis. Imagine getting paid a second income while you work at your current job, without breaking any rules or regulations of your current employer of course. If you need a little inspiration to get you out of bed each day to go work…joining out team could be just what you need!

The word "job," is an acronym that stands for "just over broke," for many people trying to make ends meet these days. You have the perfect location, the connections, possess teambuilding skills, and would probably love nothing more than to say "goodbye" to the stress of working 55+ hours per week, working 7 days a week, with little or no holidays, feeling underappreciated, and are not getting paid what you think you are worth…am I right? I can help you improve your financial condition and give you the option to say good-bye in 90-days or less. Isn't it time for a change? Join us!

TEAM – Together Everyone Achieves More

These are all examples of Referral Partnerships working together for the good of the team. T-E-A-M is an acronym for Together Everyone Achieves More! Anyone can participate, and everyone wins by joining our team and participating. Everyone contributes to the success of the team by doing their part. The more people that join our team, the more successful we all become.

To give you an idea of how powerful this could be, one retailer, Dollar General, reported on October 30, 2009 of having **8,720 store locations in 35 states.** That is more locations than giant retailer Wal-Mart! How many major retailers can you think of in your community? Imagine having one car parked in the parking lot at all times, 24/7, advertising the Dollar-a-Day Real Estate Investor Network…working to help put money in YOUR pocket each year!

Promotional Items

The Dollar-a-Day Real Estate Investor Network operates as a Real Estate Investment Training Company. We must be careful in all that we say and do, be careful not to mislead people, operate ethically, and within all legal guidelines. To do so, it is imperative to standardize all that we do worldwide, including only using high quality APPROVED promotional items. You might have the best of intentions, but adding one wrong word or phrase might possibly land all of us in hot water, from a legal standpoint. It is my intent to have most promotional items that you would need available for quick download, direct from the website.

In addition, to help keep expenses to a minimum, I will be able to take orders for promotional items from each Chapter on a monthly basis, purchase at bulk rates, and pass the savings along to each Chapter. You will have the option to purchase promotional items such as business cards, referral card invitations, frig magnets at wholesale costs. These items are all optional.

Strategies to Grow Members

There are many ways for you to build and grow your Chapter team, but I have provided a few ideas that I think will work well in any community. If you will utilize each of these methods on a regular basis, I feel you will have no problem in building a chapter with a solid membership base in your community.

Feel free to share any tips and ideas for growing your membership so that I can share with everyone in the Network. I plan on having a few sections in the Network Newsletter dedicated specifically for tips on building, growing, and sustaining your membership base. Remember, two heads are better than one, fifty is better than two, and a hundred heads are even better!

1. Direct Mail
2. Auto Billboards
3. On-line Affiliates
4. Classified Ad Affiliates
5. Community Reps

Program 1: Direct Mail

Get paid to mail out postcards! This is perfect work-at-home business opportunity for the person who prefers no people contact, and wants to work from the comfort of their own home. Your job is to mail out and/or distribute postcard Invitations to businesses and individuals in a specified target market. You will be paid a commission on any registration, membership, or product sale generated from your direct mail efforts. Each invitation will have an ID on it for tracking purposes.

2010 Direct Mail Campaigns

Campaign 1: Top 10 Military Installation households

Campaign 2: Real Estate Agents

Campaign 3: Retail Managers

Campaign 4: Cosmetologists / Nail Techs

Program 2: Auto Billboards

Your car + My sign = $$$$$$

Do you live, work, or play in close proximity to a major retailer, grocery store, convenience store, restaurant chain, shopping mall, truck stop, college campus, or other similar high traffic area? Do you frequent any of these places on a regular basis throughout the week? Do you know anyone else who does? If so, you could benefit from owning and operating a Dollar-a-Day Real Estate Auto Billboard businesses.

How does it work?

Each contractor will be registered using their name, vehicle make and model, zip code, and retail location, if applicable. Contractors will place professional magnetic signs, and/or bumper or window stickers on their car that contain our logo and website address. The goal is to park or drive where you have the most potential for people to walk or drive by and see your sign. <u>NO Selling is Required</u>. Let your Auto Billboard do the promoting, and I will take care of everything else. You might consider carrying Referral Cards with you in the event that someone asks you about it.

Objectives

1. One or more vehicles parked in every major retailer parking lot
2. Semi-truck auto billboards on every major interstate highway 24/7
3. Auto billboards on every college campuses

Target Markets

Here are some ideas to help get you started.

- Retailers: Dollar General, Family Dollar, Dollar Tree, Wal-Mart, Target, Sam's Club, Lowes, Home Depot
- Movie theatres, Starbucks, Barnes and Noble, Books a Million, Convenience Stores 7Eleven, and Circle K
- Electronics and Cell Phone Stores, such as Best Buy and Verizon Malls
- Malls: Outlet Malls, Strip malls
- Beauty care: Salons, Tanning Salons, Nail Salons, Spas
- Office Supply: Office Max, Staples, Office Depot, UPS Store, Mailboxes, Etc, Kinkos/FedEx
- Education: College Campuses, Universities, Community Colleges, Daycare Centers
- Restaurant Chains: Sit down, and fast food

This list of categories and store names is not exclusive meaning that you are free to form Referral Partnerships with anyone or for any location situated in highly visible and/or high traffic areas. No establishments of ill repute will be authorized under any circumstances. A good rule of thumb would be if you wouldn't take your mother there, I probably would not want the company name and logo parked outside there either. No Gentlemen's Clubs or sleazy dives please. Email if you are unsure.

Where to Get Your Signs

I have found the least expensive, most professional, and quick turnaround company to purchase magnetic signs is **Fast Signs, www.FastSigns.com**. You can order from them direct in person, or on-line, and have them match the logo to the paint scheme on your vehicle. I will provide you with the authorized artwork. The last time that I purchased signs, I paid $36.24 for two signs, one for each car door.

You may want to consider purchasing something for the back of your car bumper, or a window sticker or sign. We can bulk order small static clings for windows from $3-6 each, and sunshades for $10.99 each, depending on how many colors, and how many we purchase at one time.

Signs for your back rear window are also available from www.fastsigns. com, but are a little more expensive. They are see through from inside the car, but from the outside, you see the sign. I just paid $198 for one of these signs. To view, go to the website, click the "pictures," tab,

Program 3: On-line Affiliates

Have you heard stories of people making tons of money on the internet and wonder how that is really possible? More likely than not, I would bet that the majority of those people are making their money through some type of "affiliate" marketing program.

I did a Google search for the word "Affiliate Marketing," and found the several definitions and links, and pasted them below this section for your perusal. I encourage you to do your own search to see how people are using this method successfully.

Affiliate marketing is a form of marketing where individuals or businesses promote another website business for compensation. The affiliate displays a banner ad, text ad, display ad, or some type of ad on their website, blog, or internet space in view for their visitors. When one of their visitors clicks on the ad, (pay per click), or purchases something, the affiliate earns compensation for the referral.

You may not know it, but if you use the internet, you probably have been a participant in affiliate marketing. If you have done a search online, in particular, using the Google search engine, you have seen Affiliate Marketing in action. Those blue ads that are listed on the top, and on the right hand sides are all examples of affiliate marketing. Although affiliate programs may vary as to how the compensation plan works, the most common description is that a Company places an ad online, and every time that someone clicks on the ad, OR clicks, enters a website & purchases something… an Affiliate gets paid!

Affiliates have a wide variety of options to help them promote a company's products and services, such as blogs, websites, and social networking sites such as Twitter, Facebook, and MySpace. Affiliates are limited by only their imagination, which is very exciting, and just one reason Affiliate Marketing will be around for many years to come! Google Adwords, and Google AdSense is probably the most popular Affiliate Marketing Program available.

As one of our Affiliates, you will promote the Dollar-a-Day Real Estate Investment company, products and services and get paid a commission when we receive a sale from one of your affiliate links. The Affiliate software tracks and reports everything so we don't have to!

Definitions of **Affiliate marketing** on the Web:

- Affiliate Marketing is an Internet-based marketing practice in which a business rewards one or more affiliates for each visitor or customer …
- en.wikipedia.org/wiki/Affiliate_marketing
- A specialized form of marketing where an advertiser seeks to advertise or sell products or services through an affiliate network
- en.wiktionary.org/wiki/affiliate_marketing
- Affiliate marketing is a method of promoting web businesses through revenue sharing advertising between two websites. The affiliate website displays a banner advertisement of another website, to share their visitors. The affiliate in turn gets compensated for displaying the advertisement.
- www.kneoteric.com/knowledge-base/glossary/glossary.html
- A form of marketing where individuals promote a business in exchange for either a percentage of the sales they generate or a specified amount for …
- www.ultimatesitepromotion.com/free-dictionary-online-marketing-terms.htm
- Affiliate marketing is the use by a Web site that sells products of other Web sites, called affiliates, to help market the products. Amazon. …

- developer.admob.com/wiki/Definitions
- revenue sharing between online advertisers/merchants and online publishers/salespeople, whereby compensation is based on performance measures, typically in the form of sales, clicks, registrations, or a hybrid model.
- keywordmktg.com/Glossary.aspx
- this involves websites selling or promoting something from another website and receiving some sort of commission or percentage in return.
- www.onlineadvantage.co.nz/glossaryofwebterms.php
- A method of marketing where other websites can sign up to sell your products for a commission.
- www.outsource2india.com/webanalytics/glossary.asp
- A system of advertising in which site A agrees to feature buttons from site B, and site A gets a percentage of any sales generated for site B. It can also be applied to situations in which an advertiser may be looking for marketing information, rather than a cash sale. ...
- www.expedite-email-marketing.com/internet_marketing_ glossary_internetmarketingtermsdefinition.htm
- A marketing technique that uses affiliates in order to generate leads.
- www.fastfind.com/Corporate/PartGlossary.aspx
- Considered a widespread method of website promotion, affiliate marketing rewards an affiliate for every visitor, subscriber and/or customer provided through its efforts. It is a modern variation of the practice of paying finder's-fees to individuals who introduce new clients to a business.
- www.cocommunications.com/buzz_glossary.asp
- Where a company will pay a commission on any sales or registrations that are generated from another company promoting their products for them.
- www.atsf.co.uk/mim/glossary.php
- Performance based online marketing.

- www.longtail.co.za/index.php/news/whatis/online-advertising-jargon-for-dummies
- A kind of marketing program, wherein merchants pay the agents, once the visitors complete a specific action, on a Cost Per Action (CPA) basis.
- www.promotefirst.com/resources/seo-glossary/
- Affiliate Marketing is another term for CPA Advertising. This is a form of advertising where the advertiser pays based on specified actions taken by the end user. Some examples would be filling out a form after clicking on the ad or purchasing a product after clicking on the ad.
- webmastersedge.net/home/2008/defining-advertising-terms-and-acronyms-part-two/

Program 4: Classifieds Affiliates

Place our FREE E-book ads in classified newspapers online or hardcopy versions and receive commissions on any sale generated from your ad. Territories are available for American Classifieds, Penny Pincher, Thrifty Nickel, Top Military Installation newspapers, and E-bay.

A Business ad for the American Classifieds newspaper at the time of this writing is $8 for the first 10 words. There are online and print versions available.

Dollar-a-Day Real Estate Investments
Free E-book (PP31)
www.youpublish.com/NancyGaskins

Earn 10,000 in 10-days
Free E-book (PP31)
www.youpublish.com/NancyGaskins

Auto Billboard Business
Your car + My Sign = $$$
Free e-book (PP31)
www.youpublish.com/NancyGaskins

Program 5: Community Reps

Your job as a Community Rep is to promote the company throughout your community during your annual Membership Drive. The easiest, most profitable strategy would be to become a Referral Partnership Recruiter. Build a team of Referral Partnerships, and assign each team member specific objectives to complete.

- Place referral cards at designated referral locations, and keep them well stocked.
- Post referral cards or flyers on community bulletin boards
- Place referral cards next to cash register checkout counters at high traffic locations like convenience stores, beauty salons, spas, nail tech salons, restaurants, truck stops, or even post on pizza delivery boxes!
- Auto billboards at high traffic retail locations throughout the community
- Direct Mail to targeted neighborhoods and/or businesses
- Classified ads in your local community newspapers
- Host daily, or weekly Membership Info meetings

5. Show Me the Money: How do I get paid?

I offer a competitive, lucrative compensation plan, which includes a standard commission plus profit-sharing bonuses. Our books are available at over 150,000+ retailers online. Royalty payments are paid on all book sales from our publisher. Commissions are paid daily for each product or service that is sold. Commissions are paid electronically through www.paypal.com.

Sales can be generated from the efforts of Client Members located world-wide, as well as from company based advertising and promotional efforts.

1. Income Opportunities

There are several ways for you to earn income by joining the Dollar-a-Day Real Estate Investor Network. Commissions are paid on Memberships, Event Registrations, Royalty payments for books and publications, Commissions for ad space in the back of each publication, and profit-sharing bonuses for rental income.

- Referral Partnership/Affiliate Registrations

    $35 per year

    Commission: $10

    Renewals: $5   Paid Daily

- Dollar-a-Day Real Estate Investor Network Memberships

    $35 per year

> Commission: $10
>
> Renewals: $5   Paid Daily

- Books & Publications
  > We receive 20% Royalty from publisher
  > Commission: 10% of Royalty received from publisher
  > Paid Quarterly
  > Book sale referral: 40% profit sharing commission

- Ad Space Commission 10%   Paid Daily
  > Network Directory Ad Space: $50 per year
  > Sponsorship Ad Space: $10 - $100 per event
  > Corporate Contributors: $250 per event
  > Monthly Newsletters: $10 per month

- Rental Income Profit Sharing Bonuses: TBA
- Network Investor Loan Program
  > Fixed rate of return comparable to 30 year fixed rate mortgage
  > www.bankrate.com for latest quotes.

2. Guarantees

Some communities are smaller than others. Some people may be better or worse off financially. Some local economies are flourishing, while others are struggling. Some people will appreciate our concept, while others will not. There is no way for any business, including the Dollar-a-Day Real Estate Investment Company, to make any type of financial claims, expressed or implied, including any guarantee of sales or income. There are too many variable, and it is also illegal to do so.

Note

This is not a public offering. This is not an offer or invitation to sell or a solicitation of any offer to purchase any securities in the United States or any other jurisdiction. Any securities may only be offered or sold, directly or indirectly, in the state of states in which they have been registered or may be offered under an appropriate exemption.

3. How Much Can I Make?

You will receive a Financial Goals Worksheet and Referral Partnership Strategic Planner worksheets to assist you in creating an action plan to help you achieve your financial objectives based on the commission structure of the Dollar-a-Day Real Estate Referral Partnership Compensation Plan.

Although there are no guarantees of income, the following example will give you an idea of the income potential available using our marketing strategies and compensation plan for a Referral Partner Affiliate who chooses to work solo, versus one that will choose to build a team of 1 to 5 Referral Partnerships over the same time period.

# of Referral Partners	Potential Earnings
Working Solo	$ 9,841
1 Referral Partner	$59,046
2 Referral Partners	$118,092
3 Referral Partners	$177, 138
4 Referral Partners	$236,184
5 Referral Partners	$295,230

As you can see, the income potential is drastically increased as you leverage yourself and enlist the help of Referral Partners to help you achieve your financial goals.

4. Allocation of Resources

I understand that we all work extremely hard for our money, and my job is to put your money to "work" in the smartest locations possible. For investment purposes, read the Chapter titled, "Risks and Rewards," to learn my philosophies on how I will put your money to work investing in real estate by purchasing below market value, profiting from day one on each property, with *cash*, and no mortgage.

To diversify, lower risk, and to help ensure solvency and profitability, I have provided you with a variety of options to earn income. I will strive to continuously add other complimentary products and services to generate additional streams of income, such as the sale of books, publications, and special events. Should some unforeseen emergency arise, I will maintain an emergency reserve fund.

I have included the breakdown and allocation of resources for how I will financially manage the Network on the next page.

Resource Allocation

- Real Estate Investing: 60%

- Advertising/Promotion: 15%

- Management/Administration/License Fee/Product Development: 10%

- Reserves: 10%

- Incentives & Awards: 5%

The Dollar-a-Day Real Estate Investment Plan promotes and uses the following resource allocation percentages for every one dollar *loan* that is received from Client Investors. Sixty percent (60%) will be invested in real estate and supporting assets, fifteen percent (15%) will be invested in traditional advertising and promotional efforts to promote the company, products and services. Ten percent (10%) for the administration and management of the Company and Network, ten percent (10%) will be held in reserve for emergencies, and five percent (5%) will be used to recognize individuals and teams for their achievements.

To be fair, any commission that cannot be tied to a specific Affiliate, or that is generated by company advertising and promotional efforts, will be considered a team share bonus opportunity, and will be split equitably among Affiliates based on a point system and paid monthly.

6. How Do I Get Started?

Becoming a Dollar-a-Day Real Estate Investor might prove to be one of the best financial decisions you have ever made! I think you will be amazed at what can be accomplished with only a small investment of $1 per day.

1. Log on to www.iTrainInvestors.com.
2. Click on the "Member Signup" tab
3. Read the Joining Agreement
4. Fill out the Membership Application
5. Choose the Client Service (Membership) option **Associate**
6. Pay your Membership fee

** IMPORTANT **
Don't forget to click on the "Sign up to be put on email list." I need this authorization to send Monthly Newsletters, training modules, and email correspondence. Please add me to your address book to prevent my correspondence from being inadvertently placed in your SPAM folder by mistake.

What happens next?

I will send you a Client welcome letter, questionnaire, along with my contact information, including a telephone number.

We will work together over the course of the first 30-days to establish your personal goals, create a specific game plan that includes clear expectations for the upcoming year, and determine how best I can help you achieve your goals.

Together, we will schedule convenient dates and times for our client consultations, coaching, and accountability sessions, which can be by telephone, chat, email, or other agreed upon medium.

I look forward to working with you this year!

Continue reading this book to learn more about Dollar-a-Day Real Estate Investing!

7. Upcoming Investment Cycle

Now investing in residential properties in Northwest Florida, the panhandle of Florida, along the beautiful Emerald Coast of Florida: Destin, Miramar Beach, Fort Walton Beach, Niceville, Valparaiso, and Crestview, Florida

Upcoming locations: Communities in close proximity to the top 10 US Military Installations.

- Open Enrollment each quarter, closed when funded
- Goal: 12 Properties
- 3 Bedroom, 2 Bath Single Family Home
- 1,750-1,850 square foot home
- Capitalization: $100-300K per property
- Target Market: Military families relocating to or vacationing in the area
- Minimum investment: $30 per month

Coming Soon...

The Dollar-a-Day Real Estate Investment Training Program will soon be available world-wide in book form at over 150,000 retailers online, such as Barnes and Noble booksellers, www.bn.com, Amazon, www.amazon.com, and Books a Million, www.booksamillion.com to name just a few.

You have the financial opportunity of a lifetime right in front of you today! Be one of the very first people to join our team and start earning profits before the book even hits the bookstores! In addition, every time one of these books gets sold, YOU will earn a royalty payment just for being part of our team. Read on for further details on how you can benefit and profit financially from joining our team this year.

Part I

In Pursuit
of the
American Dream

The Game of Life

I read the following information recently, so I don't know who wrote it, but was blown away by its simplicity and the fact that it accurately describes what I have been teaching, coaching, & motivating people to do for years. Read it, & I think it will strike a chord with you as well...

The Game of Life

When you break down this crazy game called "LIFE," it all really comes down to two different things that drive us to get out of bed in the morning. We all want "more TIME" to do the things we love and "more MONEY."

There are generally 4 types of people in the world. What category do you currently fit in? Read on to find out…:

Category #1 – People with no time, and no money.

Most employees fall into the category. You can't go shopping on a Tuesday afternoon or fire your boss whenever you like. Most employees can't even save money in their pension to last a few years!

Category #2 – People with no time but have lots of money.

Self-employed, professionals and small business owners are in this category. They are slightly better off than the employee because they earn more, but they have to work even harder than employees to keep up with the diminishing profit margins, competition and servicing their customers.

Category #3 – People who have plenty of time, no money.

A lot people abusing the welfare system, slackers and bums have lots of time but no money. Maybe ignorance is bliss, but without a stable source of income, how long can you last many days forward?

Category #4 – Got time, and lots of money.

This is the category that big business owners, landlords, and investors are in. Imagine, not having to work for money, but having money to work for you by investing and earning profits or setting up residual "cash flow" businesses.

Short Quiz:

1 – Which one of the four categories are you currently in?
2 – Which one category do you desire to be in tomorrow?

If you consider yourself a #1 or #2 type person I'm guessing deep down you're tired of what you are doing and would enjoy and appreciate having more time and money (#4).

The only way to achieve time and money freedom is to take action and change things in your life that aren't working. So if you're currently working as an employee making someone else rich, do something about it! If you're currently working your rear off but never have any spare time to do the things you love, do something about that too!

Try something "New" today and break out of the rut! Remember...the only thing that distinguishes a "rut" from a "grave" are the dimensions!

It has been said "when the student is ready, the teacher will appear." If you are truly ready to move from either Category 1 or 2 to a solid 4...I have the ability and am willing to help you!

P.S. – If you are one of those type #3 people then this business probably isn't for you. Nobody becomes successful without drive and motivation which are key ingredients to making it BIG from home. Yes, there is actually "work" involved, but there is definitely a difference between working hard, and working smart...I will teach you how to work smart.

Are YOU Dying?

First, I was dying to finish my high school and start college
And then I was dying to finish college and start working
Then I was dying to marry and having children
And then I was dying for my children
To grow old enough
So I could go back to work
But then I was dying to retire
And now I am dying…
And suddenly I realized
I forgot to live.

Please don't let this happen to you
Appreciate your current situation
And enjoy each day

To make money, we lose our health,
And then to restore our health we lose our money…
We live as if we are never going to die,
And we die as if we never lived.

How To Stay Young

1. **Throw out nonessential numbers.** This includes age, weight and height. Let the doctors worry about them. That is why you pay 'them.'

2. **Keep only cheerful people in your life.** The grouches pull you down.

3. **Keep learning.** Learn more about the computer, crafts, gardening, whatever. Never let the brain idle. 'An idle mind is the devil's workshop.'

4. **Enjoy the simple things. The simple things are the easy things in life.**

5. **Laugh** often, long and loud. Laugh until you gasp for breath, and then laugh some more.

6. **The tears happen.** Endure, grieve, and move on. The only person, who is with us our entire life, is ourselves. Be ALIVE while you are alive. Your strength and courage will see you through.

7. **Surround yourself with what you love** , whether it's family, pets, keepsakes, music, plants, hobbies, friends, or whatever else makes you happy.

8. **Cherish your health:** If it is good, preserve it. If it is unstable, improve it. If it is beyond what you can improve, get help. And if there is no help, count your blessings and enjoy each day you have left.

9. **Don't take guilt trips.** Take a trip to the mall, even to the next county;

to a foreign country but NOT to where the guilt is. The guilt trip is a wasted trip.

10. Tell the people you love that you love them, at every opportunity. One day you may come to regret that you didn't!

AND ALWAYS REMEMBER :
Life is not measured by the number of breaths we take, **but** by the moments that take our breath away.

Credits: I received the poem above and the following advice, "How to Stay Young," as an email forward with no author listed. Enjoy!

The Dash by Linda Ellis

The following is a wonderful truly inspiring poem that fits right in with everything that I believe and promote to others. The title of the poem is "the Dash," and it is written by Linda Ellis and is available on-line in book form, or as a beautiful DVD slide show set to music, from Nightingale Conant at www.Nightingale.com. Stop what you are doing right now, go log on and watch this movie. I guarantee you that it will inspire you.

The gist is this: A man was at the funeral of a wonderful friend giving the eulogy. He remarked that the neither the date of her birth nor date of her death mattered. What mattered most was all the time spent between those years...her DASH. Only the people, who knew her best, knew what that little line was worth.

I ask you this question: If something happened to you today...would you be proud of what they say about YOUR DASH? I challenge you to forget about yesterday, and start making a difference with your DASH TODAY!

The Definition of Success

Don't be fooled into thinking that being "successful" just means "looking" successful. Just for a moment, I ask that you forget about how many "Coach" or "Dooney" bags that you have, the prestigious name brand clothes & jewelry that you wear, what kind of cool car that you might drive, all the "toys" you may have in your possession, what your job title is, or how much salary that you might make.

Success in Life

Success in life is not measured by how much DEBT, credit cards, or payments that you can rack up. You may be surprised to find out that true "Success" in life means MUCH MORE than just mere "MONEY."

Financial Freedom

Don't get me wrong, it is my opinion that everyone should strive towards achieving financial freedom. There is no doubt that having money gives a person more options in life. I don't think any of us could honestly say that we would not enjoy a few more options in life this year! :)

Having money also gives us the opportunity to help others in need, make our communities and world a better place to live. I definitely believe that "financial freedom" is a major cornerstone for success in life; but I want to warn you that you must be careful to keep it all in its proper perspective.

Strive for a Well-balanced Life

Let us strive to achieve a "well-balanced" life that will INCLUDE financial freedom, and not just use "money" as our sole definition or benchmark for achieving success.

For the record, I believe that you CAN and should strive to have it ALL... the American Dream lifestyle...remembering that there are 7 VITAL key components for success in life, and not just ONE (money). It will take all 7 to get you there, and to ensure your happiness!

Can you list the 7 Key Areas?

Rate yourself on how well you are doing in each of the categories below.

1= extremely satisfied; 2=could use some work; 3=not at all satisfied

1. **Health & Fitness**
2. **Relationships**
3. **Personal Finance**
4. **Career**
5. **Self-development**
6. **Contribution to Society**
7. **R&R – fun time**

The American Dream

Where did the phrase "the American Dream" originate?

The Library of Congress contains the original quote. The term was first used by James Truslow Adams in his book *The Epic of America* which was written in 1931. He states: "The American Dream is "that dream of a land in which life should be better and richer and fuller for everyone, with opportunity for each according to ability or achievement.

It is a difficult dream for the European upper classes to interpret adequately, and too many of us ourselves have grown weary and mistrustful of it. It is not a dream of motor cars and high wages merely, but a dream of social order in which each man and each woman shall be able to attain to the fullest stature of which they are innately capable, and be recognized by others for what they are, regardless of the fortuitous circumstances of birth or position." (P.214-215)

Apparently Adams intended "the American dream" to be one of equality across class barriers. Over the years, the definition became more modest -- a white picket fence, 2.5 kids, and a manageable amount of credit card debt.

What does living the "American Dream" mean?

The Encarta dictionary online defines the American Dream as follows:

> *"Traditional U.S. social ideals: the idea that everyone in the United States has the chance to achieve success and prosperity."*

Many consider the American Dream as the widespread aspiration of

Americans to live better than their parents did. For many, the American Dream has become the pursuit of material prosperity. These people work more hours to get bigger cars, fancier homes, bringing home the fruits of prosperity for their families. Others focus less on financial gain and place more emphasis on living a well-balanced, fulfilling life.

In Pursuit of the American Dream

Many people believe they are chasing after the American Dream to only find that they were chasing and running in the complete opposite or wrong direction. Your attitude will affect your actions, which will affect your results. It is almost impossible to be negative and move forward at the same time. I have included a few descriptions below to help you identify those people that might be hindering your success in life. Don't let them steal your dreams! Accept the fact that some people will always choose to lead a mediocre life, will resent those who don't, and move on to find more people like yourself who are ready, willing, and able to pursue the American Dream!

PS You may be shocked to hear that well-intentioned family and friends can be your worst enemies when it comes to stealing your dreams and preventing you from achieving your American Dream.

Not Me's

These people believe that successful people are somewhat different than the rest of us and possess special skills or advantages that we lack. This is ridiculous! All you have to do is find someone who has already done what you want to do and follow their steps.

Label-Mabels

I'm too busy, I'm too young, I'm too old, I'm too shy. These people do nothing but make excuses. While they are busy making excuses, you should be busy building the life you are meant to live! They will still be making excuses long after you are enjoying the fruits of your labor!

What If'ers

What if this happens, what if that happens, what if it doesn't work, what if? These people anticipate the worst in every situation. Consider this..what if something DOES happen? These people can also be worrywarts, and are constantly worrying about what other people think. Rejection is part of process of sifting through prospects to find positive, enthusiastic people with big dreams who recognize the opportunity you are offering them.

Not Now'er

These are the procrastinators in the world. They postpone attempting to go after their dreams and become successful until some event in the future will occur. When the kids go to school, when I lose weight, when I finish school, when I save enough money, when I get married, when, when, when. The right time to pursue your dreams is today, starting right now, not tomorrow of the next day!

(1) Overachievers:

Never before in the history of the United States have more people worked so hard and sacrificed so much to achieve their personal definition of "living the American Dream." Most have far more than our forefathers ever dreamed of, yet much to our dismay, those that have officially "arrived," find that they are left feeling empty and unsatisfied at the end of the day.

Another frequent problem cited is that some people work so hard for "retirement," meaning that this is the entire focus of their lives. They work 24/7 towards turning 65 or some other magical milestone. The next thing they know, they have some life altering health problem come up and realize how they have squandered their time on things that are just not that important.

These overachievers have worked so hard that they have not taken time to "stop and smell the roses" along the pathway to success. They wake up one morning to find that they have lost all that is dear to them; their relationships, youth, time, & health.

In addition, they have become so accustomed to the busy schedules required to attain or maintain their success stature, that they have NO time to enjoy their prosperity.

Point to Ponder: Do you know anyone that fits the above description?

(2) Pessimists: Winners or Whiners?

There is a distinct difference between winners and whiners. Whiners sit around and complain while winners go out and make things happen! Many people that I have encountered say and believe that the American Dream is beyond the grasp of the working class who must work two jobs to insure their family's survival. They have all but given up on even attempting to create and live the "good" life. These people go with the status quo; believe what they hear from other mediocre people, work their entire lives earning an average wage, live paycheck to paycheck, but never really get out of the rat race because in their hearts, they don't think it is a real possibility.

They tend to be extremely jealous of others because they don't realize there is more than enough resources available world-wide for *everyone* to be successful. Most do not even realize that their viewpoint is one of scarcity and not abundance; their mentality says that someone else's success take the "possibility" of success away from them. They are quick to make remarks such as these:

- That person has a lucky charm wrapped around his neck. He is the luckiest person I have ever seen!

- It takes money to make money, and I don't have any money

- They must have come from the "right" family, went to the "right" school, etc.

- She's a crook! There is no way she achieved all that legally!

- I don't know how in the world the banks keep giving them credit! I wouldn't have bought that color if someone gave me a million bucks!

- I'm doing okay; I go to work and I pay my bills and that is enough.

You can usually trace a pessimist's viewpoint back to one of two things in their life. One group doesn't believe it is possible because no one in their family or circle of influence has ever attained real success. Since this is the case, they make the incorrect assumption that it is not a possibility for them either. Remember, people tend to believe or not believe based on their own life experiences.

The second group may have tried to achieve success in the past, but failed miserably. They might have been embarrassed and vowed to never try again. They might not have had the support of their family or friends, and this failure just "proved," them right. Most people do not understand that past statistics show that it takes about **17 failures** before you finally achieve "success."

Points to Ponder: How many people in your circle of influence have truly achieved and are living the American Dream? This doesn't mean they are up to their eyeballs in debt and have tons of "stuff." Use your definition for the American Dream and see how many people you personally know that have achieved this status.

Do you have the determination and fortitude to keep trying until you make it, or will you stop after the first failure you encounter?

A Few Words About Money

Since this book is primarily all about helping you to earn a substantial amount of money in a short period of time, before we get started, I feel compelled to take a few moments of your time to discuss personal finances. Money isn't everything, until you have none. Money isn't everything, until you try to live a day without it. Money isn't everything, if you have plenty. Money is not everything; but the fact is that we cannot function in society without it. Money is nothing more than a "tool" that can be used to provide more options in life for you and your family. Money in itself is neutral, despite what some people think or say. You always have a choice about what you do with your money. You can use it for good, or you can use it for evil.

People start out in life working for their money. They go to work to earn a paycheck. If they stop working, the income stops. The goal for everyone should be to strive to become financially fit. A financially fit person is one that has attained the level where his or her money is actually working for them… rather than the other way around. For example: You have put your money to work in such a way that you *do not have to work to earn money* any longer. If you decide to not work or quit; your income level or standard of living will remain the same. Sound impossible? With a little planning and goal setting, you can be well on your way to becoming financially fit!

Remember, the goal for you if you are reading this book is for you to *"not" be average.* Despite the record breaking number of millionaires that are being made each year, the majority of Americans are anything but financially fit. Lottery winners become broke within a year or so of their financial windfall. Although many of us may have a decent source of income, we do not have the skill set or discipline to do what is necessary to become financially independent. We tend to "look" rich, but the reality is that we spend way more than we earn, we are in debt up to our eyeballs, and are less than 60 days away from bankruptcy. If you can't manage $1000 per month, you will not be able to manage $10,000 per month. The reality is that you will just be broke on a higher pay scale. Learn how to control your money, and make your money work for you… or you will continuously be working for your money! This is not a pretty picture that we are painting for our future. We are living longer than in any other time in history, and this means it is going to take even more money than before just to maintain our standard of living.

How many of you desire to work hard for 20 years or so and retire and have to live on far less than you did when you were working? Isn't that the American Dream to work your whole life and end up worse than when you started? I say this tongue in cheek, as I am quite sure this is not your definition of how you want to live your life, and hence, why you are reading this book.

Anyway you choose to think about money; the cold hard reality is that money is what makes the world go 'round. You have to have it to live, and most all the things that you want to have, be, or do, will cost money. The best not-for-profit organizations of the world still require money to provide their community services. Our churches require money. If you want to really make a difference in this world, you can bet it will take some money to help make your dream a reality! Are you convinced that money is important, or do you still need more time to decide? Let's now take a look at what part of our financial report card looks like in America.

Just what is a financial report card?

- <u>Net Worth</u>: Assets (Own) Minus Liabilities (Owe)
- <u>Credit</u>: Credit Score & Access to Money
- <u>Income</u>: Amount, Risk Factors, & Sources (Passive vs. Active)
- <u>Savings</u>: Emergency Savings, Short & Long-term Savings, Retirement Planning
- <u>Risk Management</u>: Insurance(s) to protect you against potential loss

Here are a few financial statistics from the US Census Bureau for 2006:

Personal Income by Education:

High School: $26,505
Some College: $31,054
Bachelors Degree: $43,143
Masters Degree: $52,390
Doctorate: $70,853

*roughly half of those with graduate degrees in 2005 were among the nation's top 15% of income earners.

Median Income Levels for people over the age of 25:

Males: $39,403
Females: $26,507
Combined: $28,567

US Households Income Levels
42.7%
Income: Less than $25,000

70.95%
Income: Less than $50,000

94.37%
Income: Less than $100,000

12.28%
Income: $50-75,000

16.94%
Income: $50-100,000

4.66%
Income: $75-100,000

5.63%
Income: $100,000 or more

Median Income: $46,326

Distribution of Household Income
Top 25%
$77,500 or more

Middle 50%
$22,500 – 77,500

Bottom 25%
$22,500 or Less

In a Nutshell: Welcome to the Poorhouse America!

What do all these numbers mean? It means that 94% of American households earn less than $100,000 per year, while the top 1.5% of households earns $250,000 or more. Income levels tend to be higher the more educated a person becomes. Being "average" in America means that your household earns somewhere between $22,500 and $77,500.

I gave you these numbers as only a way for you to check your current income levels against the current population in American. This is only one piece of the financial report card puzzle. I want to advise you not to get caught up in the numbers because I know first-hand from working with countless numbers of people and my own personal finances what is most important. It is *not* how much money you earn that will make a difference in your life; what matters in the long run, is *what you actually do with the money* that you have earned. You must learn how to put your money to work for you and your family if you are to ever become financially independent and achieve the kind of success that most people only dream about.

You might be surprised to learn that there are people that are literally "broke" making $10-20,000 per month. These people are no different than those that are broke making only $1,000 per month. They are just living paycheck to paycheck on a higher level. Again, it is not how much money that they make that is the problem; it is what they are doing with what they have that is the real underlying problem.

What does the word "wealthy" mean?

- Marketing companies and investment houses classify those with households exceeding $75,000 as mass affluent.

- Sociologist Leonard Beehgley identifies those with a Net Worth of over 1 million as "rich."

- Upper class is most commonly defined as the top 1% of households, commonly exceeding $250,000 annually.

Success Tip: Commit today to become financially fit. Learn what you need to know about putting your money to work so that you can achieve financial independence. Imagine what it would feel like to really **own your own life**; to have the time, money, & health to spend your time doing the things that you want, when you want, with those you love most.

Part II

Introduction & Background

Introduction
Top Questions Answered
Values
Financial Benefits
Background

Introduction

Have you ever dreamed of becoming a real estate investor, but have NO cash, credit, knowledge, experience, or time? Becoming a Real Estate Investor has never been easier or more affordable than now. The American Dream is alive and well, and can be yours in as little as 90-days from today.

Dollar a Day Real Estate Investing provides a legitimate way to work from home, earn a living, build a retirement, and be able to spend more quality time doing the things you want, with the ones you love.

Earn While You Learn

For less than the price of one soft drink per day, the 90-day Dollar-a-Day Real Estate Investment Training Program will teach you how to:

- Earn a significant amount of cash in a short period of time
- Build Residual Income
- Invest in real estate without the hassles & headaches of buyers, sellers, & tenants

It is indeed time for change in America! Together we can turn the current credit crises into an opportunity to make a positive difference in people's lives, starting with your own. Mark your calendar, 90-days from today. What's YOUR dream?

The American Dream is Alive & Well

People continue to suffer financially due to the economic crisis that has swept our nation. Jobs, income, homes, cars, and pensions may have been lost, but the American Dream is alive and well, and can be yours in as little as 90-days from today.

Dollar-a-Day Real Estate Investments is an affordable, easy to understand, 90-day program that teaches everyday people how to go from "**poverty to prosperity**," for a minimum investment of just **one dollar per day**. No minimum income, credit scores, license, or experience is required to become a Dollar-a-Day Real Estate Investor.

No hype and no fine print. For less than the price of one soft drink per day, you will learn how to earn enough cash to live life large based on your very own personal definition of what that means.

Poverty to Prosperity in 90-days

My goal was to create an affordable opportunity that can help anyone, regardless of their current socioeconomic status. Income, credit scores, bank account balances, net worth, education, experience level, or where you live will not prevent you from becoming successful. Dollar-a-Day Real Estate Investing has the potential to help those that are struggling financially; those that are doing so-so, as well as those that may already have it really "going on."

Benefits:

Read the following financial descriptions to see if you can find "yourself," in one or more categories.

- Have you been looking for a legitimate way to work from home, earn a living, build a retirement, and be able to spend more quality time doing the things you want, with the ones you love?

- Maybe you are not really all that interested in becoming a real estate investor, but want to enjoy all the benefits that real estate investing can provide, primarily financial independence.

- Are you a Retail Manager or worker that either has access to a steady client base each week, or maybe you work or live somewhere that has access to plenty of foot or car traffic? (Think shopping malls, convenience stores, grocery stores, drug stores, electronic stores, banks or ATM machine locations, big and small box retailers such as Wal-Mart, Target, Home Depot, dollar stores, hair salons, nail salons, movie rentals, popular restaurants, including franchises.

- No access to large sums of cash or credit, but would jump at the opportunity to capitalize on all the great real estate deals available in the marketplace today.

- Perhaps you may be exploring options that would enable you to earn quite a bit of cash in a relatively short period of time.

- Are you an Armed Forces service member, or family member, from any branch of the service, active duty, disabled, or retired, conus or oconus, looking for a way to supplement your current income, or retirement?

- You might be someone who has been hit hard by the current recession, looking for a way to rebuild what you have lost.

- Are you one of those that have struggled and worked hard for many years just trying to provide the basic necessities for your family, i.e. food, clothing, & shelter… only to wake up one day to find yourself close to retirement age, or yearning to retire … with no money in the bank to support a real retirement?

The point is, YOU, the person reading this page, could be anyone, anywhere in the world…the girl or boy next door, the person you pass on the highway today, the single mom at the grocery store checkout, a high school or college dropout, someone with perfect or less than perfect credit scores. You might be a person from another country, other than the USA, looking for a way to significantly improve your personal finances. No matter who you are, I believe the Dollar-a-Day Real Estate Investment Program can help you achieve your financial dreams this year and for many years to come.

Wealth Building Strategies for Everyday People

The Dollar-a-Day Real Estate Investment Program makes it easy and affordable for everyday people to invest in real estate without all the hassles, red tape, and learning curve. If you can afford $1 per day, $30 per month, you can become a real estate investor today. This program will show you specific strategies to use to turn a small investment of $1 per day into a fortune!

Dollar-a-Day Real Estate Investments is a step-by-step, "fast-track" program created specifically to help everyday people profit from real estate based on their unique financial objectives and budget constraints. No credit, income, real estate knowledge, experience, or license is required.

Each of the Dollar-a-Day Real Estate Investment Program strategies has the potential to provide you with one or more of the following financial benefits:

- Quick cash
- Fixed rates of return
- Residual income.

CASH is KING

This program does *** NOT *** contain any gimmicks, get-rich quick techniques, or "creative" financing strategies promoted in most of the real estate investment books available in the marketplace today that require specialized knowledge or skill sets such as: rehabbing, lease options, for sale by owner, rent-to-own, subject-to's, or foreclosures.

Although these techniques are being used successfully in the real estate investment business, my primary goal is to provide you with low risk, affordable options to invest in real estate to secure your financial future.

The Dollar a Day Real Estate Investment Program competitive advantage is that we use the power of our *people network* to negotiate and purchase real estate properties for CASH. We pay for our investments with cash, no mortgage payments, and therefore, have no fear of foreclosure to prevent us from sleeping well at night.

If you can make a commitment to consistently invest just a few hours each week to building your business, and can afford $30 per month, ($1 per day), less than the price of one soft drink per day... you have the ability to significantly increase your financial well-being this year by becoming a Dollar-a-Day Real Estate Investor.

In as little as <u>90-days from today</u>, *using the Dollar-a-Day Quick Start Guide, you can be well on your way to living the life of your dreams!*

Summary

Isn't it time that you quit trading your time for dollars? Work-from-home with a flexible work schedule, get paid extremely well for RESULTS, instead of hours worked.

This program has the potential to help you earn enough money to help you make ends meet, get out of debt, significantly improve your quality of life and lifestyle, spend more time with your family & friends, QUIT your day job, RETIRE... OR achieve WHATEVER lofty financial goals you may have.

Here's what you will learn:

(1) How to earn a significant amount of cash in a short period of time, passive or active participation, working part-time

(2) Strategies to fund your own real estate investments, or other business venture with CASH, and no credit.

(3) Options to offer or receive a fixed rate of return to you and/or your investors.

(4) Create a stream of residual income that will keep paying you month after month...for the work you perform only once.

Congratulations!

Congratulations on your choice to improve the quality of your life and lifestyle this year by reading this book and learning more about becoming a Dollar-a-Day Real Estate Investor! Feel free to email me your comments, suggestions, and recommendations on how I can serve you better or improve the Dollar-a-Day Real Estate Investment Program, and this publication.

I look forward to hearing about and sharing your success story in future editions.

To Your Success!

Nancy Gaskins
the Dollar-a-Day Real Estate Investor
www.iTrainInvestors.com

Keywords:

Self-Help
Real Estate
Investing
Real Estate Investing
Real Estate Investor
Personal Finance
Money
Wealth Building
Entrepreneurship
Work-at-Home
Retirement
Business

Company Overview

The Dollar-a-Day Real Estate Investment Company is a private real estate investment training company. Our primary strategy is to buy residential real estate at a significant discount, with CASH. We then fix them up and rent or sell to private individuals. We finance our deals with private funds from Investors in our Private Investor Network that are looking for the (a) high returns, (b) positive cash flow, or (c) residual income that real estate investing brings, as well as proceeds from the sale of our training products and services.

Business is Booming

The home-based business trend is booming, real estate investment opportunities are more than plentiful, and the Dollar-a-Day Real Estate Investment Training Program can show you how to take advantage of both of them so that you can take control of your future, your finances, and your life!

Bank on Yourself: Finances, Family, Freedom

My goal is to teach others how to duplicate the "Earn as You Learn," Dollar-a-Day Real Estate Investment Program and use as a way to secure their financial futures. I can show YOU how to do the same.

Live Your Life Exactly the Way You Want

- Set your own schedule
- Skip the commute and work from home
- Spend more time with family & friends

Benefits of Joining our Team:

- Active or Passive Role, your choice.
- Work from home, start today! Great home-based business opportunity.
- You are in charge of your own business, flexible schedules
- Work solo or as part of a team, your choice
- Unlimited earnings potential; get paid for results rather than hours worked
- Wouldn't it be nice to know you are in a place where you are recognized for your achievements?
- Are you ready to have fun while creating the life you've dreamed of?
- Can you imagine being in a positive environment where you can make a difference in people's lives?
- 200-300% higher returns than CD's, mutual funds, bonds or money market
- Low Risk with well secured Real Estate as collateral
- Hassle free; No credit, income, license, or experience required to participate as a Dollar-a-Day Real Estate Investor
- Affordable, monthly payment plans begin at only $1/day, $30 per month

Top Questions Answered

1. Description
2. Eligibility Requirements
3. What help will I get?
4. How do I find customers?
5. How much does it cost to start?
6. Are there other costs involved?
7. How do I get paid?
8. How do I get started?

Dollar-a-Day Real Estate Summary

Description

The Dollar-a-Day Real Estate Investment Company is a private real estate investment and training company. The Dollar-a-Day Real Estate Investor's primary strategy is to buy residential real estate at a significant discount, with CASH, then fix them up, and rent or sell to private individuals. We finance our deals with private funds from Investors in our Private Investor Network that are looking for the (a) high returns, (b) positive cash flow, or (c) residual income that real estate investing brings, as well as proceeds from the sale of our training products and services.

My goal is to purchase a minimum of 10-12 properties per year. I offer a convenient, affordable option for everyday people to invest in real estate for only $1 per day. I am able to provide this service at this low cost per month because the Dollar-a-Day Real Estate Investment business model is based on team-based management principles, building the company through the use of Referral Partnerships located throughout the world.

I teach my Clients how to duplicate the Dollar-a-Day Real Estate Investment system as an affordable way to achieve financial independence.

Eligibility Requirements

No credit, income, experience, knowledge, or license is required to participate as an Investor Trainee. You can live anywhere world-wide and join our company. There is a minimum legal age restriction for those that wish to participate as Level I, II, or III Investors.

What Will I Learn?

Dollar-a-Day Real Estate Investor trainees will learn how to identify, select, make offers, raise investment capital, purchase, and manage real estate investment properties for cash flow and profit. Dollar-a-Day Real Estate Investing will teach you how to create and implement "systems" that will enable your real estate investment company to operate on auto-pilot, helping you to make more money in less time and with less effort.

Other benefits include a listing in the Network Directory, access to on-line discussion forums, marketing materials, world-wide advertising & promotion, network management & administrative support, and Dollar-a-Day Real Estate Products and Services.

In addition to becoming a Dollar-a-Day Real Estate Investor, you may decide to partner with us and use our company as a home-based business to generate income for your family. Who do you know that would enjoy the opportunity to increase their income this year?

Use the training manual to help you create a plan to reach your financial objectives for the year. Use the Dollar-a-Day Real Estate wealth-building strategies, and recruit Referral Partnerships anywhere world-wide to exponentially increase your income this year.

You can pick and choose which strategies that works best for you; it might be something as simple as a magnetic sign for your car door, mailing out postcard invitations, handing out a referral card, or tweeting online! The strategies you can use and have at your disposal are only limited by your imagination!

How Much Does It Cost?

The annual enrollment fee to register as a Dollar-a-Day Real Estate Investor Network Member is $35 per year. Tuition and Network access is $1 per day, ($30 per month). Level I, II, and III investment programs are $30, $50, and $100 per month respectively.

Client Membership is limited and by invitation only. Chapters will be authorized on a first-come, first-serve basis. To avoid market saturation,

Chapter and enrollment authorizations will be based on population and housing trends in the area. Membership drives will be conducted only one time per year in each community. Fees are for a 12-month period and will not be prorated.

Are There Other Costs Involved?

There are NO additional costs involved to become a Dollar-a-Day Real Estate Investor, other than the fees listed above, depending on which client program you choose. You do have the option to purchase marketing and promotional items at wholesale cost.

How Do I Get Paid?

I offer a competitive, lucrative compensation plan, which includes a standard commission plus profit-sharing bonuses. Commissions are paid daily for each product or service that is sold. Sales are generated from the efforts of individual Referral Partnerships located around the world, as well as from company advertising and promotional efforts.

A fixed rate of return that is comparable to the current 30-year mortgage rates offered in the US is available to those that choose to participate in the fixed rate loan program option.

To be fair, and to promote working as a team, any commissions that are earned by company advertising and promotional efforts, as well as Rental Income profits generated will be split equitably among all active Referral Partners. Commissions that can be tracked to an individual Referral Partner will receive the entire commission.

In addition to becoming a Dollar-a-Day Real Estate Investor, you may decide to partner with us and use our company as a home-based business to generate income for your family. Who do you know that would enjoy the opportunity to increase their income this year?

Use the training manual to help you determine your financial objectives for the year, use the Dollar-a-Day Real Estate wealth-building strategies, and recruit Referral Partnerships anywhere world-wide to exponentially increase your income this year.

You can pick and choose which strategies that works best for you; it might be something as simple as a magnetic sign for your car door, mailing out postcard invitations, handing out a referral card, or tweeting online! The strategies you can use and have at your disposal are only limited by your imagination!

How Do I Get Started?

You can initiate Membership registration directly from the website, www. iTrainInvestors.com. Your application will be processed immediately upon receipt.

Values

Before we get started, I want to share with you the specific traits that I value and am looking for in the people that desire to join our team. I deem it important to know something about a person's character and thought processes prior to joining forces, so I will also share some of my personal philosophies that I feel most strongly about to help aid you in your decision. This will save us both a lot of headache and heartache and will let you know right up front whether you will be a good fit for the company, and vice versa.

Some of my philosophies: God first, family & friends second, career third. It's not a sin to be rich or wealthy, I think it's a sin to be poor. Do what you love, love what you do, the money will eventually follow. It's okay to fail, it doesn't mean you are a failure. If at first you don't succeed, try, try again.. and again, and again! Get up one more time than you fall down. Learn from your mistakes and the mistakes of others. Your starting point doesn't matter, its where you end up that makes the difference. If you want what you have never had, you have to do what you have never done. Quit doing the same thing over and over again expecting different results. Don't settle for mediocrity, strive for extraordinay. Remember that it's just the little "extra," that you do, that will take you from ordinary to extraordinary! Lead by example, follow the golden rule, and understand that we ALL have areas in our life in need of improvement, some more than others. Be open to new ideas and willing to step outside your comfort zone to achieve success. Don't be afraid to admit you have made a mistake and ask for forgiveness. Forgive others.

One of my favorite quotes is from Master Motivator Zig Ziglar, and I try to live by this credo:

"You can have anything in life that you want, as long as you help enough other people get what they want"

Traits:

1. Positive disposition
2. Honesty
3. Integrity
4. Self-motivation
5. Ambitious
6. Good communication skills
7. Professionalism
8. Willingness to learn and be coached
9. Willingness to make business a priority

Imagine this...

Can you imagine how exciting it will be to have the opportunity to... work with, brainstorm with, coach, be coached, share success stories with, and just hang out and have some FUN with... a group of people that ALL possess these traits? I am looking forward to it and can hardly wait to meet you!

*** Fast-Start Bonus Opportunity ***

As a thank you for being one of the first to purchase and read this program, I would like to help jump start your real estate investment career and help you be one of the FIRST to profit from the program. You are eligible to have your name, contact information, and state, listed as a <u>Dollar-a-Day Real Estate Investor</u> in the Investor Directory Section of the Dollar-a-Day Real Estate Investments book. Participation is limited and is based on a first-come, first-serve basis. There are two primary advantages to having yourself listed: (1) Earn referral commissions, and to (2) Attract potential investors for future projects.

Earn Referral Commissions

Dollar a Day Real Estate Company operates strictly from REFERRALS ONLY. Just like most credible direct sales companies, the only way to join our company is BY INVITATION ONLY, from another Dollar-a-Day Real Estate Investor Network Member. Timing is everything, and this could be the opportunity you need to jump start your business with very little effort on your part! Imagine waking up tomorrow morning and receiving an email notice that money has been deposited into your checking account simply because someone saw your name listed as a referral partner and used **your name** as a referral source!

Attract Potential Investors

Another very important reason to advertise is to also provide you with a forum to help you attract potential investors to fund your real estate projects. Should you decide to build your own real estate investment company and need help financing your portfolio purchases, it is imperative to have a quick way to locate and connect with people who are interested in what you have to offer. You can easily create a webpage that you can list each of your projects, along with the details. Prospective investors can view what you have to offer and contact you for further details.

No Unfair Advantages

To be fair to everyone participating, and to prevent anyone from having an unfair advantage simply because their last name, state, or city they live in begins or ends with a certain letter of the alphabet, your information will also be posted to our online Directory, and can include a photo for FREE, and will rotate on a continuous basis. Participants will be able to click on your link to give you credit for the referral.

To Advertise:

Updates will be made to the Directory on a calendar quarter basis, once every three months. To advertise to a world-wide audience in every single book that is sold, you can have your name and contact information added to the print and online Directory, at the introductory price of only $30, which equates to $10 per month for the opportunity to have a world-wide audience at your disposal.

This introductory offer is limited and will be restricted to the first 500 applicants, and will be accepted based on a first-come, first-serve prepaid basis. You can apply to advertise for 1,2,3 or 4 quarters. I will keep a waiting list and you will be notified if and when I have an advertising slot open.

This book and directory will be made available world-wide at more than 150,000 book retailers online, such as Barnes and Noble Booksellers, www. amazon.com, in addition to other major retailers that have a web presence and sell books online.

Deadline	Quarter
December 1	January – March
March 1	April – June
June 1	July – September
September 1	October - December

To see an example of the professionalism, world-wide distribution, marketing and promotions of my life enrichment book series titled: In Pursuit of the American Dream, feel free to GOOGLE my name, "Nancy Gaskins," or the title of book one, "Live Like You are Dying: How to Transform Your Life in 30 Days," or simply go to any major player in the book industry, such as Barnes and Noble (www.bn.com), Amazon (www.Amazon.com), and type in my name or book title.

In addition, you are eligible to become one of the first to receive a 20% discount and autographed copy of this program in paperback book form once it becomes available from the publisher. Anticipated retail price is $15.95. Email nancy.gaskins@operationHSH.com to be placed on the list. Bulk discounts are available for those that desire to become distributors.

I welcome your comments and suggestions for improvement to this manuscript.

Background

The Dollar-a-Day Real Estate Investment Program was originally created in an effort to provide financial solutions for military families world-wide, primarily as an opportunity for military spouses to work from home, earn a decent income, and fund their own personal retirement plan.

While working on this program, I was faced with a crisis of my own. My husband became seriously injured while downrange in Iraq. It became evident that our military career would be cut short, several years ahead of schedule. Our financial future and fate will be solely determined and dictated by a Medical Board, and not by either one of us. That is a terrifying fact all by itself. Knowing that you have absolutely no control over the outcome is stressful to say the least. Our children are all grown, and I am able to provide income for my family, thank the good Lord above; but I can't help but think of all those families who are not as lucky. It could be worse, no doubt, but it certainly could be a whole lot better.

This program is not just for military families, this program is for everyone. I have included information on how this program can benefit you if you are a military or civilian family. I have learned that we ALL have a story, and I hope that the Dollar-a-Day Real Estate Investment Program can help provide you with enough financial capital to ensure a happy ending for yours!

How many times throughout the years have you paid rent, or drove past a subdivision and wished that you could own just a little piece of it? Dollar-a-Day Real Estate Investing can help you turn that thought into a reality this year. Join Today!

Nancy Gaskins,
The Dollar-a-Day Real Estate Investor

Military Spouse Retirement Program

One of the most difficult things faced by our military spouses is the fact that it is almost next to impossible to create and build a successful career that is flexible, mobile enough to take with you anywhere world-wide, and provides an opportunity to fund a retirement that is comparable to that of our military spouse counterparts.

OCONUS Opportunities

My stint being stationed in Europe opened my eyes to another widespread problem faced by military families overseas. Due to strict regulations, income earning opportunities for spouses abroad is practically non-existent. What could be considered as a dream assignment could certainly be made much sweeter if only these spouses had a legitimate way to earn a few extra bucks each month. There is tons of untapped entrepreneurial potential inside these spouses. It is such a shame that there is no legitimate outlet for them to share their gifts and talents! Now there is…welcome!

Armed Forces Retirement & Savings Plans

Most military families have no idea the real financial value of their military retirement plan. I often hear complaints about only receiving 50% of their base pay after 20 years of service. They feel it's unfair and not enough. I tend to ruffle some feathers in the room when I ask the question, "How long do you think it would take you to save a half a million dollars, or $500,000 dollars? Could you do it?" Most of them in the room think that is an absurd question. I then explain that number is just about how much it would take to provide you with about $25,000 income before taxes, or $2.083.33 per month, earning 5% interest per year…about what some of their retirement checks would be each month!

Although the military retirement plan is quite good in my opinion, and we now have another option the Thrift Savings Plan, (TSP), both of those are probably not going to be good enough if you didn't start soon enough. Most of us do not like the idea of decreasing our standard of living, by losing 50% of our income…most of us would much rather have 100% or more if given the option. Am I correct?

The War in Iraq Creates Financial Distress

A much more urgent "quick financial solution" for problems being faced by my immediate family and so many of my extended military families around the globe was desperately needed, and forced me to realize how important this project was, and that it was even more IMPERATIVE that I finish, and make it available as soon as possible. Extensive injuries received from the war in Iraq have put many families in financial jeopardy almost overnight, including my own.

Armed force members have been forced to medically retire without much warning and <u>without</u> solid information to make informed, sound, financial decisions. Many of our families are now, or soon will be without any or enough financial wherewithal to adequately take care of their families. Almost overnight, these families have the potential to lose half or more of their paycheck, along with their benefits. On top of their disabilities, no matter how many contingency plan B's or C's one might have had in place…I have found no legitimate resources, tools, or programs available to help people recover quickly from a huge financial downturn.

Government bureaucracy is full of red tape, this problem is new, they are learning as they go along, and military families have become the guinea pigs. This not meant as a derogatory statement against the government, or the military, as they are not set up or designed for this purpose. I am a very proud US Army wife of many years. With that said, the fact is that our families require assistance NOW, rather than later, and we have no time to WAIT on the government to fix our financial problem.

I absolutely refuse to stand by and watch my family, or any other family become a "financial" casualty, when there is a simple solution available. I opt to use my education, experience, compassion for others, and my desire to live the American Dream as a platform to inspire others to regroup, refocus, get back to the basics and come to rely on what originally and continues to make America great, "life, liberty, & the pursuit of happiness."

Families Need Opportunity, Not a Government Handout

I saw a bumper sticker on a window the other day that sums up my feelings regarding most any type of governmental handout: "Your fair share is NOT in my wallet!" The solution to any of our financial problems as families, communities, nations, or to the world is NOT a government handout, but an "opportunity." The best way I can explain it is by using a verse from the *Holy Bible*, "give a man a fish, feed him for the day; teach him how to fish, and feed him for a lifetime." The government handouts are the equivalent of "giving a man a fish, feed him for the day." Guess what? Tomorrow that very same man or woman will be hungry once again, and will be back knocking at your door asking for another fish, rather than going out and catching one himself!

Governmental or any type of "free" handout or subsidy "enables," people, rather than provide them with the resources or tools needed to help themselves. Instead of becoming productive members of society, if we are not careful, we will create a nation full of lazy people who can't think for themselves or problem solve, doing nothing all day long but having one gigantic pity party, feeling sorry for themselves, standing around with their hands out, waiting for the free check to be deposited into their bank accounts each month, complaining all the way to the bank about why they don't have it any better than they do. Blah, blah, blah.

I don't say any of this to offend anyone, and I need to make it very clear that I do believe in helping those that are less fortunate, and understand that we all have a moral obligation to do so. My statements are to raise awareness and provide a solution to prevent this type of "somebody owes me," mentality to infect out nation any more than it already has. You can read more of my thoughts in this section under the caption, "Challenge to Succeed 2010: How to Transform America One Family at a Time,"

Recession Hits US

Families across America are experiencing the same "type" of devastating financial losses that my military family friends were experiencing...almost overnight. People are losing their jobs, their incomes, their homes, their cars, their pensions, their families, their health, and underline everything that symbolizes the American Dream.

Fundraiser Edition:

My book series is designated as a **Fundraiser Edition**, which means the sale of this book can be used as a way for any private organization or charitable group to raise funds. Your group can purchase these books in bulk, at wholesale cost, and sell them at retail for fundraising purposes. Another option is to become an affiliate, put my link on your website, blog, newsletter, etcetera, and get paid a commission when someone purchases as a direct result of your referral. To register your group for a fundraiser, email Nancy.Gaskins@operationHSH. com, and give me your details. Beginning in 2010, your fundraiser can also be listed on my website.

You may not have purchased this book; you might have borrowed this book from a friend or the library, or even received it as a gift, and would like the opportunity to make a difference. You can help in several ways: Make a cash donation, purchase this book, (keep one, give another away to a friend,) join our team, or simply help me spread the word and forward the information to your friends and family members.

The Solution

I soon realized that the financial program that I was creating for military families, the Armed Forces Real Estate Program, if tweaked just a little, had the potential to benefit millions of American families, and thanks to the internet, families located around the world!

Millions of people are searching online for legitimate, work-at-home business opportunities. This clearly demonstrates to me that the American Dream is alive and well, and there are still plenty of people out there pursuing it, despite all the doom and gloom that is being reported by the media and critics.

"Home ownership" is by far one of the most important cornerstones that most people use to gauge how close they are to living the American Dream. By using what we know about the current state of the economy, the real estate market, and by listening to what people are looking for, I was able to come up with an <u>affordable option</u> for everyday people to invest in real estate to get ahead financially. These options have the potential to

(a) Earn participants a significant amount of cash in a relatively short period of time…which will provide much needed cash flow on a daily basis to help make ends meet

(b) Adequately fund real estate portfolio purchases… for <u>CASH</u>

(c) Provide a fixed rate of return to participants and their investors

(d) Create a stream of residual income that will keep paying you month after month…for the work you perform <u>only once.</u>

Mission

My MISSION in life is to inspire, educate, & motivate individuals to create and live a well-balanced life filled with purpose, achievement, and financial prosperity.

My Message

I believe in the "American Dream" and what it stands for: the idea that EVERYONE has the chance to achieve success and prosperity. I believe this dream can be extended to include ANYONE world-wide. If you can "dream" it, with a little effort on both our parts, I can help you "achieve" it!

The American Dream is still very much alive and well within YOUR reach, despite your past or present circumstances. Allow me the honor to help you clear the path this year so that you can follow your heart and begin living "the DREAM."

"In Pursuit of the American Dream" Book Series

The name of my life enrichment book series is "In Pursuit of the American Dream," and you can easily identify it by the American Flag and the Statue of Liberty book cover. Another distinguishing mark is the "Support the Troops," yellow ribbon in the top right hand corner of each book, designating each one of my books as a Special Edition in which part of the proceeds is used to support our American Military Families around the globe. Each book is also available and designated on the back cover as a fundraiser Edition for clubs, organizations, and other groups to use to raise funds for their organization, membership, or for families in financial need.

You may purchase any of my books at a 10% discount, direct from me by visiting my website, www.NancyGaskins.com, or go to any of the 150,000+ online retailers world-wide, such as www.bn.com, (Barnes and Nobel booksellers), www.amazon.com, or others that carry books. Enter my name, "Nancy Gaskins," as the author and my books will show up in the query. Feel free to Google my name or company name to locate news about me, my publications, and companies. Should you decide to become a distributor, or register your organization for a fundraiser, you will have the option to purchase books at wholesale, and sell them retail.

Book One recipient was the wonderful Fisher House Organization in Landstuhl, Germany. We should never forget that the American Dream would not be possible if it were not for the selfless sacrifices made by all those US Armed Forces Members and their families who have served and continue to proudly serve our great nation. All gave some, but some gave ALL.

Are you looking for a book and complete turn-key program that has the power to jump-start or turbo-charge your life? In **Book 1:** ***Live Like You Are Dying,*** I help you transform your life in 30-days by teaching you a life management system that will help you get from where you are, to where you want to be...all in record time. As George Straight, country music legend put it so eloquently, "there's a difference between living and living WELL"...how are you living these days?

*Coming Soon...*Join us in 2010 for the Challenge to Succeed Competition, where our goal will be to "transform America, one community, neighborhood, family, person at a time!" Go to the appendix in this book, OR Log on to www.NancyGaskins.com OR email nancy.gaskins@operationHSH.com for more details on how you can register yourself, family, friends, church family, organization, or neighborhoods for the Challenge to Succeed 2010 Competitions for Life!

In **Book 2:** ***Dollar-a-Day Real Estate Investments***, I have created an investment program that makes it easy and affordable for everyday people to invest in real estate without all the hassles, red tape, and learning curve. If you can afford $1 per day, you can become a real estate investor! This book contains strategies for turning your small investment into a FORTUNE.

Each of the Dollar-a-Day Real Estate Investment program strategies has the potential to provide you with one or more of the following financial benefits:

- quick cash
- fixed rates of return
- residual income

This book specifically teaches you how to earn the money required to negotiate and purchase real estate properties for cash. Pay for your investments with cash, no mortgage, and no fear of foreclosure!

Join me on my quest to build the largest, most profitable real estate investor network in the nation!

PART III

Establish Your Financial Objectives

Chapter 1
Determine Your Financial Objectives

Each of the Dollar-a-Day Real Estate Investment Program wealth building strategies in this book have the potential to provide you with one or more of the following financial benefits; quick cash, fixed rate of return, and residual income.

A variety of factors such as your personality, time constraints, financial budget, and financial goals will determine which strategies you will want to use in your new real estate business venture.

Any goal not written down is merely a wish. I'm sure you may have heard that before, but it is true. How can you hit a target that you cannot see? I think and do things a bit differently than most. I ask everyone involved in the Network to establish their financial objectives for the year, quarter, month, and week and submit to me for my planning. I use YOUR numbers to establish MY financial goals and targets for the company. Working as a team, we will craft a variety of strategies that will enable all of us to reach our desired financial objectives. A true win-win solution for all of us involved in the Network!

Before you can decide on which Dollar-a-Day Real Estate program and strategy(ies) to implement, it is important for you to determine your specific financial objectives for the upcoming year. I encourage you to read this book from cover to cover to explore all the financial possibilities available before you make up your mind on what you can or can't do. Don't place limitations on what you would like to accomplish financially. It is amazing what people can accomplish when they have the right kind of motivation, inspiration, and team available to support them.

You will need to complete this exercise in order to map out a strategy that will help you meet your financial targets for the upcoming 90-days.

Feel free to change, elaborate, add, or delete objectives based on your personal financial preferences. You must put a specific dollar amount and clear description for each objective so that you can later create a plan that will enable you to achieve your financial goals for the year. If you do not know how much something will cost, you must research on-line, or go window shopping to give you an estimate to use for your worksheets. Use the examples on the next page to help you get started.

To get you started thinking about your financial future, read the following general statements to help you become very clear on what you want to accomplish, financially speaking. Keep this in mind as you read about the benefits each of the Dollar-a-Day Real Estate Investment Program strategies can offer you this year.

General Financial Objectives & Recommended Strategy:

1. I want to earn extra cash just to help make ends meet each month (Strategy 2)

2. I have a pressing financial situation that will require me to earn a significant amount of cash in a short period of time. (Examples: Pay off mortgage, student loans, fund a real estate investment portfolio or college fund.) (Strategy 2)

3. I hope to become debt-free, or I want to save for a short-term goal such as a vacation, send my kids to camp, purchase new furniture, or save for a down payment on a car. (Strategy 2)

4. Replace or increase my current income so that me or my spouse can afford to: stay at home, quit our day job(s), or retire. (Strategy 2 & 3)

5. I prefer to earn a fixed rate of return on my investments. (Strategy 1)

6. Make a major contribution to society; financially support a cause that is dear to my heart. (Strategy 1,2,3)

7. My goal is to drastically improve my personal finances and create a lifestyle for my family that most people will only dream about. (Strategy 1,2, & 3)

Examples

I want to earn extra cash just to help make ends meet each month
Revised: **I will net $250 extra dollars each month to be used for groceries.**

I have a pressing financial situation that will require me to earn a significant amount of cash in a short period of time.
Revised: **I will earn $15,000 no later than (date) to pay legal expenses.**

I hope to rid myself of debt, or simply want to save for a short-term goal such as a vacation, send my kids to camp, purchase new furniture, or save for a down payment on a car.
Revised: **I will earn $47,000 no later than (date) to pay for the following:**

    a. $10,000: pay off note for 2009 BMW 325i
    b. $ 5,000: purchase new Ashley king size bed & mattress set
    c. c. $ 3,000: purchase 1.5 carat diamond ring from Tiffany's
    d. d. $ 2,000: pay off Visa credit card
    e. e. $ 5,000: Cruise to Bahamas for anniversary
    f. f. $ 2,000: Family vacation to Disney World
    g. g. $20,000: Purchase Harley Road King for husband.

Replace my current income so that I and/or my spouse can quit our day job(s)
Revised: **Earn a passive income of $125,000 per year after taxes.**

I prefer to earn a guaranteed fixed rate of return on my investments.
Revised: **Invest $30 per month, & earn a minimum 5% APR guaranteed.**

My goal is to drastically improve my personal finances and create a lifestyle for my family that most people will only dream about
Revised: Have fun with this one! Be specific on where you want to live, what kind of home you want, what kind of cars do you want to drive, vacations and places you want to travel, volunteer or philanthropic causes you want to support, clubs you want to join, schools or classes you want to attend, skill sets or things you want to learn.

Summary

People don't plan to fail; they simply fail to plan! Be crystal clear on your financial objectives and what you want to accomplish this year. Plan your work, and work your plan. Keep score of your progress along the way. The more specific that you are, the more likely you are to reach your target. You will never hit a target you cannot see.

My financial objectives for the upcoming year:

Directions: List each of your financial objectives, and use the recommendations on the previous page to identify which specific strategy is best suited and recommended for each specific type of financial goal. Circle the strategy(ies) available for each financial objective.

Count how many times you have circled each of the strategies, and write your answers in the blanks below the chart. This will help you decide which Dollar-a-Day Real Estate Investment strategies you must learn and implement to attain your financial goals this year.

We will use this information at a later time to help you create a personalized investment plan using each of the strategies.

Objectives

1._____
Strategy 1, 2, 3

2._____
Strategy 1, 2, 3

3. _____
Strategy 1, 2, 3

4._____
Strategy 1, 2, 3

5._____
Strategy 1, 2, 3

Strategy 1: _____
Strategy 2: _____
Strategy 3: _____

PART IV
Wealth Building Programs

Program 1: Low risk options for a fixed rate of return

Program 2: Earn a considerable amount of cash in a short period of time

Program 3: Create a stream of residual income that will keep paying month after month… for the work you perform <u>only once</u>

Note

This is not a public offering. This is not an offer or invitation to sell or a solicitation of any offer to purchase any securities in the United States or any other jurisdiction. Any securities may only be offered or sold, directly or indirectly, in the state or states in which they have been registered or may be offered under an appropriate exemption.

Chapter 2:
Dollar-a-Day Real Estate Program Overview

I am on a quest to build the largest, most affordable, profitable, private real estate investor network in the nation beginning June, 2010.

The concept is simple, inexpensive to implement, does NOT required any special training, license, or skill set, but will require small, consistent effort for a period of no less than 90-days from each participant.

I have included general details regarding each of the following Dollar-a-Day Real Estate Investment Programs in this chapter:

1. Low risk options for a fixed rates of return

2. Earn a considerable amount of cash in a short period of time

3. Create a stream of residual income that will keep paying you month after month… for the work you perform <u>only once</u>

Program 1
Low risk options for a fixed rate of return

The Dollar-a-Day Real Estate Investment Company promotes using strategies that enable the Investor to earn large sums of cash in a short period of time, for the purpose of improving financial and personal lives. Although you may, or may NOT have enough cash to finance your real estate purchases, it may make more sense financially for you to use private funding as a source to fund your real estate investments, and allow the rental income that is generated from the properties to make monthly payments to your lenders.

I have included information from both the Investor and Borrower's point of view, and details on how you might use the Dollar-a-Day Real Estate Investor Network as a strategy to improve your personal finances, or to help someone else improve theirs.

This program provides a fixed rate of return for participants who wish to become a <u>Program 1 Investor</u>. Affordable, monthly payment plans start at only $1 per day, $30 per month, with a minimum investment contract of $500 per year.

I understand how hard you work for your money. To minimize potential risks, investments in this Dollar-a-Day Real Estate Investor Network are "loans," secured by real estate investment properties.

How YOU Earn : Network investors will receive a **promissory note** for their loan, and will receive a **fixed rate of return** on their deposits. The APR (annual percentange rate) of return will be comparable to a 30-year fixed rate mortgage rates offered in the United States as listed on www.bankrate.com. Investment cycles begin each quarter, and end upon project capitalization. There may be higher interest rates available, depending on the project.

Why is this important?

Legally, should the company experience unforeseen financial difficulties and become insolvent, "creditors" must be paid FIRST, before any money is distributed to "investors." In this program, you are one of our "creditors." You serve as our lender, loan us money to conduct our real estate investment business, and we are required by law to pay you back, including the interest specified in your promissory note, which is a legally binding contract.

The Power of a Team

Most people would laugh out loud, and call you crazy if you told them you were interested in becoming a real estate investor, but had only $30 a month available to invest. $30 a month from only one person won't get us very far, but multiply that $30 per month times 50, 100, 1000 or more and you can begin to see how powerful only $1 per day can truly be!

By working together as a team, the Dollar-a-Day Real Estate Investment Company will be in a powerful position to negotiate and purchase properties for CASH. Rental income generated from the properties will be used to pay back the investment loans provided by members in the network, the Dollar-a-Day Real Estate Investor clients. In essense, the investors in this network are serving as our bank.

There are a variety of reasons why an Investor might choose to use private lending sources to fund their investments, rather than a traditional lending sources, such as banks:

- When time is an issue

- When privacy is an issue

- When ease is an issue

- When the amount is an issue

- When credit is an issue

- When foreclosure is an issue

- When self-employment is an issue

- When a short-term loan is an issue

- When a commercial property is an issue

- When the property itself is an issue

Due to the poor economic state of our nation, lenders have clamped down hard on investors, making it next to impossible to have quick access to cash OR to qualify for multiple loans. The loan process can sometimes take "months," rather than "days" to get an approval notification.

By using private lenders, we have quick access to an almost unlimited amount of cash reserves, which will enable us to make more offers, more often. By making more offers, it makes sense that more of our offers will be accepted. One of the biggest headaches and heartaches experienced by a SELLER is when a deal falls through because the BUYER was unable to obtain financing within the specified amount of time stated on the contract.

One of our biggest advantages will be that we have easy access to cash, and will be able to offer a seller a quick closing date. This is sure to put the Dollar-a-Day Real Estate Investment Company at competitive advantage in the marketplace!

Why Use Program 1? This program is perfect for the person who wants a low risk option that will provide a fixed rate of return that produces more income than CD's (Certificates of Deposit), Savings Accounts, Money Market Accounts, and Treasury Notes. You may not want to own and operate a home-based business, or get involved in any day-to-day real estate transaction activities, but would like the opportunity to profit from the Dollar-a-Day Real Estate investment activities.

Private Mortgage Lending VS Traditional Investment Options

These loans are very safe because they are backed by actual collateral – the real estate property. To further enhance the safety of your principal, these loans are typically made for less than the appraised value of the property. If need be, we can sell the property and easily recoup our principal.

In comparison to other investments, such as Savings Accounts, Certificat of Deposits, (CD's), Money Market Accounts, etcetera, your returns are also much higher. Go to www.bankrate.com to view the current interest rates offered on investor deposits.

Convenient, monthly payment plans make it affordable for most anyone to get started as a Dollar-a-Day Real Estate Investor. Other investment vehicles typically require a large outlay of cash or credit line, secured by personal assets, large monthly payments, and you must qualify based on income, credit scores, net worth, etcetera. For less than the price of one soft drink per day, you can become a real estate investor!

Summary

Dollar-a-Day Real Estate Investors in this network receive a fixed rate of return on their deposits. Investors have the option to make weekly,(Saturdays), bi-monthly,(1st & 15th), or monthly (on the 1st) deposits, and will receive a promissory note, with a fixed rate of return specified on your contract. Minimum investment is $30 per month, $500 total for the year. Additional deposit increments are available in multiples of $25 only.

To get started as an Investor, goto the Dollar-a-Day Real Estate Investor Network website, www.iTrainInvestors.com, and register today!

Program 2
Earn a considerable amount of cash in a short period of time

Work-at-Home: Have you been looking for the perfect (i.e. legitimate) work-at-home business opportunity? You can choose to work part-time, full-time, set your own schedule, get paid for results rather than by the hours that you work, choose what methods fit your personality, AND you have the potential to make an unlimited, almost insane amount of money should you desire to do so!

Your financial future is your responsibility, it's all up to you, and I am here to offer it to you for less than the price of one soft drink per day! Opportunity awaits you, right here, right now, for only $1 per day. Where else can you own and operate a business with this much potential, AND invest in real estate for $30 per month? Most people waste more on pizza, lottery tickets, and nonsense items each month, when they could be using that money to help them achive financial independence.

Although Dollar-a-Day Real Estate Investors can profit by participating in each of the three Dollar-a-Day Real Estate Wealth Building Programs, this particiular program provides the most lucrative opportunity for financial gain.

It should excite and liberate you knowing that you have the opportunity to quit trading your time for dollars, and get paid for what you are really worth! Lucrative financial opportunities are currently available and are earned on merit, based on your individual results, those of your team, & and results of the company. You can choose to work solo, as an active or passive participant, or leverage yourself and your income earning potential by becoming a leader and building a team to help you achieve your goals. My hope is that you are serious enough about your financial future that you will join our team and I will be writing YOUR personal success story in the next book, slated for fall 2010!

Power of a Team

There are currently 306 million people in the US, and 105 million households in America. The Dollar-a-Day Real Estate Investment Programs are not restricted to just the United States of America. That increase our market size potential to **6.7 billion** people in the world!

How many of these people do you think would be interested in learning how to legitimately increase their bank account balances over the course of the next 90-days? How many people do you think would love the opportunity to "cash in" on the current real estate crises if they had half a chance? How many people do you personally know that could answer YES to that question?

How long do you think it would take to contact 105 million households in America if we start tomorrow?

If I was the only one available to do this task, it would take me a lifetime (or it would seem like it anyhow,) as well as a hefty bank account to finance the project. But if I was lucky enough to enlist the help of 100 people today, and each person agreed to tell just 3 people, and asked each of those people to do the same, would you believe it would take **less than 10 days** to notify each and every household in America if we did it by snail mail, i.e. United States Postal Service?

Another option could possibly only take just a few short minutes, rather than days, or a lifetime, as in the scanario above. What if we enlisted the help of just a few people, and employ the most powerful tools that we have available to mankind right now...the power of the internet, email address books, and our social networks! I'm sure you have heard the saying, it's not WHAT you know, but WHO your know that counts. In the year 2010 and beyond, it's not who YOU know, but it's *who everyone else knows* as well, that will make a difference!

Have you ever watched a video on www.YouTube.com and seen how in just a matter of a few hours, sometimes minutes, the number of views quickly can skyrocket in the millions? What about email forwards? Facebook or Twitter updates? Google AdSense? BuzzAgent? Have you heard of "Pay Per Click," or making money through Affiliate Marketing? These are prime examples of viral marketing at its finest. With just one push of the "send" button, blog post, or twitter update...and a few forwards later...literally millions of people worldwide have access to the latest news and **have the ability to respond almost instantaneously!** It works just like the grapevine, and spreads just as fast as celebrity gossip!

The Stats: www.answers.com, the worlds leading questions and answer site reported that 32 million people from around the world visited Twitter in April. Only the top ten persent do about 90% of all the tweets! When I typed in the question, "How many people have facebook accounts?" The reply came back, "about 50 million people." I don't know the date on that, but no matter, it's still a huge amount of traffic and potential candidates for our program!

To put this all into perspective, imagine you have about 50 million people all in one room. You have the opportunity to step up on the platform, and use the microphone to make a special announcement. All ears and eyes are on you, and what you have to say. If you have something worthwhile to say, they will all stay tuned in, and run out and tell everyone they meet; if not, they will ignore your message. Get the picture? This is extremely powerful stuff!

Both of these strategies (offline & on-line) have a proven track record for success. A major benefit of on-line marketing is that it works 24/7 and has the potential to spread like wildfire across the world in a very short period of time, and it takes very little cash to make it happen. How exciting might this become for you as an investor or home-based business owner? Imagine if just a tiny fraction of those people joined our investor network or purchased one of our publications? How many new clients or sales would it take to finance YOUR dream lifestyle?

Quick Cash in Slow Times

By working together on a part-time basis, I can show you several affordable strategies, in addition to the ones listed above, that have the potential to provide you with enough cashflow that will help you pay your day-to-day living expenses, in addition to funding your very own real estate investment company, OR could provide you with enough cashflow, which could lead to replacing your current income, propelling you into an early retirement should you desire to do so!

Imagine having the ability to quickly earn enough cold hard cash to pay your bills, become totally debt-free, & still be able to purchase enough investment properties that will provide you and your family with thousands of dollars of cash flow each and every month! Would you be willing to trying it out for the next 90-days?

90-Day Success Formula

To keep overhead low, and to provide each of the Dollar-a-Day Investor Networks with the highest possible returns, in the quickest time possible, the Dollar-a-Day Real Estate Investment Company operates strictly from REFERRALS.

The Dollar-a-Day Real Estate Investment Program is a great concept, and offers a quick solution to a severe problem currently being faced by millions of people world-wide; a <u>lack of cashflow or money in the bank.</u> Research indicates that most Americans live paycheck to paycheck, and are less than 60-days away from bankruptcy. **How long would your finances last if you or your spouse lost your job this week?**

Your Success = Company Success

YOUR success will determine my success, and the overall success of this company, which means we have a symbiotic relationship and are dependent upon one another for success. Although I believe great real estate deals can be found in any market, I think an unprecedented number of millionaires will be made over the course of the next two years by those that are willing and able to take advantage of the current real estate opportunities that are available.

Business is Booming

The number of foreclosures posted are still at record levels throughout most of the country. This is the opportunity of a lifetime for real estate investors. The positive side to all of these foreclosures and real estate crises is that people are getting out from under homes they can no longer afford, and into homes they CAN afford. All these people still have to have a place to live, so there is ample opportunity for a win-win for everyone involved. Investors can profit by purchasing real estate at bargain prices, and those that have been displaced can afford higher quality properties or "more house" for less money.

Investors that can afford to act NOW have many more options and properties from which to choose, i.e. the cream of the crop, so to speak. If we are forced to wait, we can still be successful, but it would be like having to dig around at the bottom of the barrel to find just one good apple. Timing could possibly mean the *difference between earning thousands, or earning millions of dollars* to use to build our portfolios. Bottom line results could be determined by something as simple as how *quickly* we can get the word out to people, and how quick they will respond and accept our invitation to join our team and become a Dollar-a-Day Real Estate Investors. Your 90-day window of opportunity starts ticking the minute you finish this sentence. What's YOUR dream?

Unwritten Goals are Merely Wishes.

You can't deposit "dreams or wishes" into your bank account each week. It's imperative and mandatory that everyone turn in their personal financial goal sheets each week, month and quarter. I will use these to establish financial goals and expectations for the company.

If everyone does their part, working together, we can earn enough cash to fund our real estate investments for the quarter, and provide enough cash for everyone in the network to meet their stated financial objectives. Remember the acronym for the word TEAM. Together Everyone Achieves MORE. After we have a few weeks under our belts, we will be able to better predict our financial outcomes based on past results. I will keep everyone posted on our results via weekly email updates.

The Snowball Effect

It all boils down to a numbers game; the more people that know about our programs, and keep hearing about our program, the more likely we are to have new people join our networks.

When more people join our networks, or purchase our products and services, we will have access to more CASH, and will be able to take advantage of the great deals available in the marketplace today by having the ability to make more cash offers.

We can then purchase more properties to put in our investment portfolios, which means more rental income will be generated, more returns on investments paid to investors, and more profit sharing bonus checks that will be deposited into YOUR bank account each and every month!

The Bottom Line

Our primary objective is to get the word out about the Dollar-a-Day Real Estate Investment Program as quickly as possible over the course of each 90-day period. Marketing experts say that if people don't hear from us at least once per month, they will forget we exist. I have a direct mail, email campaign and newsletter planned that will help us to stay in contact with our potential prospects. The timing might not be right "today" for a person to join our network, but maybe in a week, month, or next year… the timing will be perfect and they will decide to join our team. I want to make sure they have that opportunity in front of them each month, and hear all about what we are doing for ourselves, others, & our communities!

No Hard Core Selling Required

Your job in this network is to promote our company, the Dollar-a-Day Real Estate Investment Company to others by using one or all of our inexpensive marketing promotion strategies. Choose whichever strategy(ies) listed below that work best for you, based on your own personal preferences, budget, and comfort zone. There are options that are sure to suit most anyone.

Preferences Examples:

1. I am a silent investor; I'll chip in, you do the work, & give me a financial piece of the profits

2. I prefer NO people contact whatsoever

3. I enjoy getting out in public and meeting new people

4. I enjoy and am comfortable socializing and navigating on-line

How You Get Paid

Every time someone joins the Dollar-a-Day Real Estate Investor network or a product gets sold, a commission is earned by the person or business that referred them, and credit is given to the network team that generated the sale. Every time we collect rental income from a property that we have purchased, profit-sharing cash bonuses are being earned by those in the network!

Referral Fees can be gained through using a variety of strategies, such as referral cards, direct mail, online advertising, websites, affiliate programs, and directory listings, to name a few.

To ensure integrity, every application or sales invoice must contain the referral source prior to processing. The referral source can come from an individual referral partner, coop advertising effort, or from the company's advertising and promotion campaigns.

Commissions generated from coop advertising efforts will be divided equitably among those participating in coop advertising that month. Sales commissions generated from company efforts will be divided equitably among all Referral Partners.

Commissions will be paid daily, electronically upon receipt via www. paypal.com. Due to the high volume expected, I anticipate that we will eventually have to move towards a standard weekly paycheck cycle, designating Thursdays as the payout day for commissions earned.

Can you imagine just how many people would love the opportunity to improve their personal finances this year?

Summary

If you have been looking for a legitimate home-based business opportunity that has the potential to help you improve your personal finances this year, as well as the opportunity to join a team that will enable you to surround yourself with positive-minded, ambitious, goal-oriented, people that place a high value on helping you achieve your goals in life, I invite you to join our team!

To join our team, visit the website…www.iTrainInvestors.com.

Program 3
Create a stream of residual income that will keep paying you month after month... for the work you perform only once.

The beauty of the Dollar-a-Day Real Estate Investment Programs is each one of them has the potential to provide you with recurring, residual, passive income long after your initial work has been completed. I am sure you are most familiar with songwriters, actors, authors, & sports heroes receiving royalty checks from their music, movies, books, and product endorsement sales years after they have actually done the work, and even after their deaths! These are all examples residual income.

I'm not against earning some good, honest, "one-shot" linear income, i.e. work one hour, get paid for one hour... but given a choice, which would *you* rather do: work hard and get paid only once, through linear income, or get paid continuously - perhaps for years or even the rest of your life - for hard work you perform only once, through residual income?

Royalty Payments

One of our primary promotion strategies is publishing books that describe in detail the Dollar-a-Day Real Estate Investment Program, and the success stories of people in our investor network. Our book(s) are published and made available in a variety of formats, such as: paperback, hardback, e-book, through email as a word document, and in the future, if all goes as planned, on CD/DVD. Books will be made available world-wide at over 150,000 retailers on-line, such as www.bn.com, and www.amazon.com!

Consider this fact... just by enrolling in the Network, and doing nothing else...you are eligible to receive a thank you cash "gift" electronically deposited into your bank account each quarter! Every time one of our books is sold... cha-ching, just like magic! You get paid, over and over again!

Dollar-a-Day Real Estate typically receives a 15-20% royalty on net proceeds from our publisher each calendar quarter for book sales. For example, if our book retails for $15.95, we will receive $3.19 on the sale of each book that is sold at full retail price, or twenty percent of whatever wholesale cost our publisher charged the book reseller, such as www.amazon.com, etcetera.

What this means is that once the book is published, as long as you remain enrolled as a Dollar-a-Day Real Estate Investor, you are eligible to receive profit sharing bonuses via royalty check distributions each and every quarter that sales are reported by our publisher!

Rental Income

Once we pay CASH for our real estate properties, they will continue to generate rental income *month after month*, unless we decide to sell and purchase something new.

After all expenses have been paid each quarter, including any investor loan payments, a percentage of profits generated from each of the properties in our portfolio will be earmarked for distribution to each of our active participants enrolled in our program in the form of a BONUS.

Once the investor loans have been paid back, the rental income will continue, and the profits will continue to pass right on through to the investors in the network! As long as you remain enrolled in Program 2, you are eligible to participate in the profit sharing bonuses.

Team Share Bonus Details

Profit-sharing (team share) bonuses will be distributed to each active participant in the Program 2 Network each quarter based on reaching specific financial milestones. Team share goals and payouts will be listed on the website each quarter beginning April, 2010. You must be an active participant in order to receive payments in any quarter. The percentages will be calculated and distributed based on individual, team, and company wide effort.

Summary

Dollar-a-Day Real Estate pays top commissions daily, weekly, and quarterly, based on both personal and company team efforts. We pay leadership and profit sharing bonuses based on how well we do as a company team in meeting our monthly and quarterly objectives in each network.

Program 2 participants are eligible to receive referral commissions on sales, royalty payment distributions, and team share bonuses.

By enrolling and becoming a registered Dollar-a-Day Real Estate Investor Network Member, you are entitled to receive royalty payment distribution bonuses each quarter on *Dollar-a-Day Real Estate Investments* book sales.

PART V
Risks & Rewards

Real Estate Investor Basics
Risks & Rewards of Business Opportunities

Chapter 3:
Real Estate Investor Basics

Risks and Rewards

As with any business, no matter how great it is, there can never be any guarantees for sales or profitability simply because we never truly know whether people will actually buy our product or service. There is no such thing as a "guaranteed sale" until (a) you have actually made the sale, (b) the money is deposited, and (c) the funds have cleared your bank…end of story. If anyone tries to tell you otherwise…run as fast as you can!

Entrepreneurs take calculated risks when they create products and/or services that they hope will provide a viable solution to a current problem in the marketplace. They "win," or are rewarded when the marketplace responds, and is willing to pay the entrepreneur for her efforts, comes in the form of a "sale," with the goal of providing a profit.

Real Estate is no different. The Dollar-a-Day Real Estate Investment Company is not different. Each comes with their own set of inherent risks and rewards. The real estate market has recently taken a nosedive in most areas across the nation. In my opinion, one of the reasons for the real estate bubble crises was because some very basic principles of "investing" were ignored or disregarded. Investors and lenders took high risks in hopes of a huge return… they miscalculated and lost. So did the rest of the nation.

There are risks associated with purchasing real estate as an investment, but as Dollar-a-Day Real Estate Investors, I have some specific ideas on how we might work together to minimize some of these risks. A typical rule of thumb for investments is the higher the potential reward, the higher the risk factor.

Since most of you reading this book will probably be first-time investors, the following strategies should serve us well:

1. Purchase properties for CASH, with no mortgage, therefore NO RISK of foreclosure and losing our properties.

2. Profit from day one, don't rely on market appreciation to give you a return. Purchase properties at least 20% BELOW market value when possible.

3. Diversify and have multiple streams of income coming in from different sources. Do not rely solely on rental income to provide returns on investments

There has never been a better time than now to become an investor. The market offers plenty of properties from which to choose, there are more sellers than buyers...which means NOW is the right time to buy.

Leverage

One of the most talked about benefits of investing in real estate is the advantage of using "leverage." No other investment vehicle allows you to put only *20% down* or less of your own hard-earned cash, and finance the remaining 80%, let somebody else make your payment in the form of rental income, which will eventually pay for your investment, and hopefully provide you with a reasonable return on your investment through appreciation. In addition, real estate typically goes "up" in value (appreciates), although Uncle Sam allows us to "depreciate" our investments on our tax returns, which gives the investor a nice tax break.

All these benefits are contributing factors to why investing in real estate is such a big deal, why so many people want to do it, and why real estate investing is still one of the top strategies used for everyday people to become extremely wealthy in a relatively short period of time.

How Lenders Minimize Risk

When lenders only fund 80% of the value of the home, they have a 20% buffer for market fluctuations. Should something go wrong with the borrower's ability to pay, and a foreclosure must occur, they have enough wiggle room, even if the market fluctuates, to sell the property and pay off the mortgage loan and foreclosure expenses with no problem.

On the flip side, if a person has at least 20% cash invested in a property, they will do whatever that is in their power financially, to keep that property from going into foreclosure. They do NOT want to lose their investment. If a person gets into a home for zero or little down…what have they invested? Zero. It's not hard to walk away from an investment when you have nothing to lose except "face," and a scar on your credit report. Make sense?

Point to Ponder: How many "no money down" opportunities have you heard of over the past few years? How many foreclosures are bogging down our legal systems and financial institutions?

Profit from Day One

Many investors make the mistake of purchasing a property for full price, or sometimes an inflated price, in high hopes that the property value will increases enough to give them a nice return on their investment. Some investment strategies rely solely on appreciation for success. I think that is a big mistake.

The Dollar-a-Day Real Estate Investment Program does not use "flipping properties," as a primary investment strategy. Flipping properties is where an investor purchases a property; rehabs, or "fixes it up," waits for the market to adjust, then sells for what she hopes will be a nice, hefty profit.

Although many have successfully used this strategy, the Dollar-a-Day Real Estate Investment Program was created for everyday people, and not market speculators. This type of strategy is too risky for beginning investors.

If you are interested in this type of strategy, I would suggest that you do a lot of research, engage yourself in some high quality training materials from experts in the field, befriend a highly recommended home inspector in your local area, find a mentor that is a successful rehabber, and agree to be an apprentice for awhile. If you have never watched the movie, "Money Pit," go rent it to find out what kinds of problems you might run into with a rehab project.

Dollar-a-Day Real Estate Investors should never rely on market fluctuations as an investment strategy. You can't deposit, "hope the property values go up," into your bank account each month. Think of appreciation as a BONUS.

Purchase BELOW Market Value

If you have the goal to purchase properties BELOW market value, you will go into the investment with a profit or what investor's call "equity." This is the difference in what the property is worth, and what you paid for it. If you will adhere to this formula… normal, small fluctuations in property values will not make a significant difference in your financial wherewithal. If you have a spike in property values, you have earned yourself a nice bonus!

No credit, creative genius strategies, or experience required

It is next to impossible for individuals to qualify or obtain financing for real estate investment projects. Most lenders will authorize a loan for a home purchase, but will not authorize more than 3 loans total, due to the risk factors involved. Everyday people are just not able to qualify for traditional loans for investment purposes due to primarily a poor financial scorecard: i.e. net worth and creditworthiness.

Simplified definition of Net Worth: Market value (what you could get if you had to sell them today) of Assets (cash in bank, savings, autos, property, etc.) that legally belong to you whether paid for or not, MINUS any debt that you owe, whether it is against one of your assets of not. What you own, minus what you owe…look at the situation below.

Look how easy it is to become upside down, in the negative!

Assets:
Cash in Bank:500
Car: 10,000
Motorcycle: 5,000
Total Assets: $11,000

Liabilities (Debt)
Credit Card debt: $10,000
Car loan: $7,000
Student loan: $30,000
Total Liabilities: $ 47,000

Net Worth: ($36,000)
$11,000 Assets Minus $47,000 Liabilities = ($36,000)

Smart people have come up with innovative ways to finance their real estate investments. There will always be people that have money or credit lines, and those that do not…the "have's, versus the "have not's."

The classic wise saying: "He who holds the purse strings, controls the world," is still as relevant today as it was years ago. Those that have financial resources are continuously looking for ways to grow their money, and are usually looking for an <u>above average</u> return on their money; else they could just put it in a savings or money market account. Again, this is a classic example of a problem identified in the marketplace, and entrepreneurial thinkers have come up with a solution, and are profiting from it!

Information Overload

There are many kinds of methods of creative financing strategies available today, and innovative people are continuously improving upon, and coming up with even better solutions for investors on a daily basis. Some are legitimate, some are not, and some are more risky than others. The choices are mind boggling. The bookstores are filled with these books, on-line chat forums are buzzing about them, and with just one keyword search on Google, your eyes may begin to cross or glaze over due to information overload!

No Get Rich Quick Formula

Although people have been, and continue to be successful using these creative financing strategies, the Dollar-a-Day Real Estate Investment Program prefers to keep our strategies simple and straightforward, and allows anyone, over the age of 18, regardless of financial report card status: (cash in bank, credit score, or net worth,) to participate and profit.

What's a "Fair" Return on Investment?

To keep current on what is going on in the marketplace each day, you can go to <u>www.bankrate.com</u>. At one glance and a click of the mouse, you can easily see and track the current 30 and 15 year mortgage rates, credit card rates, new and used auto loan rates, certificate of deposit rates (CD), Money Market Account rates (MMA), etcetera. This is a great resource that can give you a good idea of what is going on in the financial marketplace both nationally and locally by zip code.

Based on what I just read today…

People with good credit are paying on average 5.16% for a 30 year mortgage loan.

Banks are paying people 1.75% to deposit their money into a Certificate of Deposit. Let me ask you a question: Will you please loan me one of your hard earned dollars for 12 months, ONE entire YEAR, and let me pay you back the dollar, plus less than TWO PENNIES in interest? Oh, and by the way, I might mention that the prices of everything that you can expect to buy over the course of the next year will increase by at least 3 pennies on each dollar. Does this sound like a great investment plan to you?

Taking Charge of your Personal Finances

I would like to recommend that you start taking charge of your personal financial report card, beginning today. For many people it may be difficult or even a bit scary to sit down and see it on paper, in black in white. It is what it is, and until you know the facts, and exactly what you are working with, you can't expect to become financially fit.

Treat your personal finances like it was a <u>business</u> and you are the CFO... the chief financial officer. Start with a spending plan (budget,) manage your cash flow (paycheck to paycheck) to make sure you don't have too much month left at the end of your money. Make absolutely sure your business is making a profit, and that the financial choices that you are making are actually increasing your net worth, rather than decreasing it. Work on increasing your credit score to 720.

Retirement Simplified

So just how does one retire and never have to work again? Forget about winning the lottery...there are several legitimate strategies will enable you to afford to retire, and the Dollar-a-Day Real Estate Investment Program can help you achieve retirement status in record time!

- One way is to work for a company for a specified number of years, and earn a pension. An example of this would be someone retiring from the military after 20+ years of service. Service members are not required to pay in one dime, but due to their time and grade in service that are able to receive a nice retirement check once they have completed their contract period.

- Another option is that people pay into some type of retirement fund, such as an IRA, they may or may not receive some type of tax benefit from doing so, the money may grow tax deferred, and the person will be able to take it out and use it once they reach the ripe old age of 65.

- Some employers offer a retirement plan for their employees. Employees have a specified amount deducted from their paychecks, and some employers may even match the employees' contribution. If you are self-employed you also can set up a retirement plan for you and your employees.

- Entrepreneurs have the option to grow a successful business, sell it or take it public, invest the money, and retire from the proceeds.

- Consistently make sound investments over the course of a lifetime, enjoy the benefits of compound interest, and live off the interest and appreciation earned.

- Although important for financial planning purposes, some incorrectly think that Social Security is a retirement fund. Your employer is required by law to withhold 7.65% of your pay, and pay a matching 7.65%, and remit to the government on your behalf, up to a certain amount each year. It is imperative that you check your report and make sure that all your income is being reported correctly. This could affect your benefits in the future. Go to www.ssa.gov for more details.

Social Security is not ALL that

Unfortunately, most do not know that the people that have consistently worked their entire lives, who have earned a nice salary, paid their taxes, will be receiving a much LOWER social security check than those who have not worked. It's true; you are being penalized and subsidize those who have not contributed on an equal basis. I am all for helping out the poor and needy, but I do not support the lazy…and this is a severe flaw in our system. Just be prepared to be disgusted when you start hearing about the differences in social security check distributions. If you do not believe me, go to the website and read the details!

A really great resource is the www.kiplinger.com website. This easy to understand and navigate site is filled with great resources to help improve your personal finances. They publish a monthly magazine that is excellent, and is worth much more than the cost of the subscription.

How Much Will it Take?

Go to the www.bankrate.com website and see how much you can get for your money these days. For the sake of simplicity, let's say that you would like to earn $50,000 a year, before taxes, during retirement. Let's also assume that you don't have an employer sponsored retirement plan, you are starting from ground zero, and you desperately want to retire this year. Just exactly how much money, investments, or assets will it take for you to SAVE or accumulate to get you into the ballpark so you can retire this year?

Money Market Account
APR: 1.182%
Amount Required: 4.23 Million

Certificate of Deposit
APR: 1.75%
Amount Required: 2.86 Million

Real Estate
APR: 5.16%
Amount Required: $968,992

It will take roughly $968,992, invested and earning a return of 5.16% per year, to provide you with an income of $50,000 before taxes if you choose the real estate option above as your investment strategy. Are you ready to get started?

When would you like to retire? ☺

_____

Date

Chapter 4:
Risks & Rewards of Business Opportunities

Would you rather have 1% of 100 people's efforts or 100% of your own effort?

Choose wisely as it will seriously determine your success and ability to achieve financial and time freedom at some point in your life. IF you choose <u>1% of 100 people</u>, you have correctly identified one of the key tactics that the Dollar-a-Day Real Estate Investment program will use to build the largest, most profitable real estate investor network in the nation! This same tactic can be used to help YOU fund your very own investment company.

Remember our previous example of "How long would it take me to notify 105 million households about the Dollar-a-Day Real Estate Program?" If I was personally responsible to notify each household, one strategy I might use is to mail out one postcard to each of the households in America. I estimate that it would cost me about fifty cents each, for a grand total of $52.5 million dollars. Ok, wait here while I go get my checkbook...Sounds ludicrous, right? I might be lucky enough to be able to afford to mail out 100 postcards each month.

What if instead of "me" trying to tackle this impossible goal, I were to enlist the help of 100 people, and ask them to mail out 3 postcards each, and ask those recipients to do the same, and so on and so forth...the task would be much more manageable, affordable, and more likely to get accomplished, don't you think? The $52.5 million dollar direct mail bill now becomes only $1.50 each, which most anyone can easily afford, but the potential for financial rewards are much higher for everyone involved!

Learn to Work Smart, not Hard

By working together as a team, we are able to accomplish what was once thought to be an "impossible" task. Instead of only 100 people being notified about the investment program, now 103 MILLION people know about the program!

What about profits? Let's estimate that we will get a 1% response rate. For the 100 postcard mail out, that would be 1 person out of every 100 would purchase our book or join our network. Out of the 103 million households, a whopping 1.03 million would respond! A significant difference don't you think? Less effort from everyone involved, but a major difference in results! Do you agree we should learn to work smart, not hard?

The Dollar-a-Day Real Estate Investment Program will teach you how to use free to low-cost strategies that will help you to work smart, not hard.

Work-from-Home: Do you have what it takes?

Would you like to spend more time with your family and friends, doing what you want to do, rather than slaving away for some employer, trading your time for dollars? Job satisfaction, having control over your schedule and your life, being paid by how much the market is willing to pay you for what you produce, not by how many hours you put in, and the opportunity to gain financial independence are some of the top reasons many people consider self-employment opportunities. Gaining financial independence has the potential to improve the overall quality of your life and lifestyle. In the long run, you should expect to experience more happiness and joy in your life than ever before.

The "right" business opportunity can provide you with all that, and then some! With the current job market in the United States being so terrible, it has never been a better time to consider working for yourself. There has been a large upward trend, especially among women, over the past few years as more and more people are deciding to give up their daily 9 to 5 grind, to join the ranks of those of us who have decided that there must be a "better way," to earn a living, and we think it's called SELF-EMPLOYMENT.

The Risks

We have discussed some of the rewards of being self-employed. Now it is time to give you a reality check on what it really means to be "self-employed." It means you don't get paid unless you or your team produces results. It means you don't have any time clock to punch, but you have to be a self-starter and willing to do whatever it takes to get the job done. If something doesn't work, it's your fault. If something does work, it's your fault. You must learn how to work smart, not hard. You are responsible for paying your own taxes, and keeping good bookkeeping records. You are responsible for making sure your business is profitable by keeping your expenses to a minimum. You are responsible for keeping your customers and/or employees happy. There are no guaranteed customers or guaranteed sales. Do you have a spouse or significant other who will support your self-employment endeavor? Do they understand the risks and benefits? Will there be stress? Yes. Can you handle it? Only you can be the judge of that.

Quotes to Enjoy

I have a few quotes that I would like to share with you in closing out this section.

We all know, or have heard of people who may be financially successful, but have a horrible life. Many people use this as their excuse why they don't want to be financially successful. I hope you will chuckle as much I do every time I recall the famous saying…

"Money may not be everything, but it sure makes being miserable a whole lot more tolerable!"

Life is a banquet, and most poor souls are starving to death! Mamie

PART VI

Getting Started
90-day Fast-Track Guide

Chapter 5:
90-day Fast-Track Guide

The Concept

Dollar-a-Day Real Estate is a real estate investment company that provides an affordable, convenient option for everyday people to invest in real estate for only $1 per day, $30 per month. Dollar-a-Day Real Estate Investing is one of the few businesses where you can earn as you learn, right from the start.

Invest in real estate without all the hassles and headaches of buyers, sellers, and tenants. No minimum credit score, income restrictions, real estate knowledge, experience, or license is required to participate.

Investment Goals for the Network:

of Properties:
Purchase 12 properties per year

Use:
Residential Rental & Vacation Use Property

Specs:
3 Bedroom, 2 Bath Single Family Home
1750-1850 square foot home
Less than 5 years old

Median Price: $212,300

Target Market
US Military Families and/or
Families making between 80-120% of median income
Median Income: $59,000
30-35% for Rent

Location: Within close proximity (less than 15 miles) to top 10 military installations.

Exploring Your Options

Option 1: Affiliate, Passive

You can join the Dollar-a-Day Real Estate Investor Network, pay your monthly Management Fee, I do all the work, and you will get a portion of any profits earned each and every month.

By working together as a team, pooling financial resources each month, the Dollar-a-Day Real Estate Investment Company will be in a powerful position to negotiate and purchase properties for CASH. Rental Income generated from the properties, any product sales, and royalty income will be divided equitably among the group participating in the form of profit-sharing bonuses.

Option 2: Affiliate, Active

Dollar-a-Day Real Estate Investment Company operates as a referral based business. Become a Referral Partner Affiliate, and I will teach you how to earn enough money to finance the life of your dreams in as short of time as 90-days from today. In addition to earning income as a Referral Partner, you are also eligible to participate in profit sharing bonuses as stated in Option 1.

The beauty of this option is the unlimited income earning potential that is available. Your earnings are a direct reflection of your effort. You can work the program once and quit after you have reached your financial goals, or you can choose to repeat the process over and over throughout the year. As a Referral Partner, you are simply introducing the company to others as an affordable option for them to reach their financial goals for the upcoming year, and teaching them to do the same.

Most professional direct selling companies, real estate offices, hair salons, and spas operate much the same manner. Independent Reps, also known as distributor, associate, consultant, agent, member, or business owner, partner with a company that provides a product or service, along with administrative and marketing support. With the company taking care of the back end of the business, you are free to focus on the frontline actions that produce income.

What makes this so attractive is that is costs almost nothing to start and very little to run. There is no huge up-front capital investment required, so you can own your own business without having to borrow capital. There is no ceiling on what you can earn, and you don't have to sacrifice family and friends to join the highest of achievers.

Most work from home, and they work it around their everyday life. You may opt to use this business to supplement the household income, and continue in traditional employment. For others, this business may be used a sole source of household income. The point of Dollar-a-Day Real Estate Investing is to provide freedom and flexibility to fit your personal ambitions and circumstances. What counts is that you get to decide what's best for your life.

Management Fees

The following is a breakdown of how the Management Fee is calculated and spent each month.

Investing: 60% - $18.00
Advertising/Promo: 15% - $ 4.50
Administration: 10% - $ 3.00
Reserves: 10% - $ 3.00
Incentives: 5% - $ 1.50
Total: 100% - $30.00 per month

Investing: Sixty percent will be allocated for investment purposes. Rental income generated will be divided equitably among those in the network.

Advertising/Promo: Fifteen percent will be allocated to advertising and promoting the Dollar-a-Day Real Estate Investment Company, Investor Network, Products, and Services.

Administration: Ten percent will be allocated for the day to day operation and management of the company.

Reserves: Ten percent will be allocated for legal, accounting, insurance, and emergency fund use. Each property that is purchased will have a minimum of 3-6 months (depending on the current market conditions) of expenses held in cash reserves to cover potential emergency expenses and any holding costs associated with potential vacancies.

Each month, ten percent will be budgeted for repair & maintenance, housekeeping, landscaping, and insurance expenses.

Incentives: Five percent will be allocated for professional development, recognition awards and bonuses for top business builders (Referral Partners) in the network. Everyone in the network wins financially when the membership grows, so we will provide this additional incentive.

Option 3: Investor

As a Dollar-a-Day Real Estate Network Investor, you will not have all the hassles & headaches of buyers, sellers, and tenants. Your investment is structured as a "Loan" that we use to purchase real estate investment properties. I will pay you a fixed rate of return that is comparable to the current 30-year fixed rate mortgages offered by top financial institutions. Go to www.bankrate.com to view the latest rates.

☑ It's Your Company, Let Your Voice Be Heard

My goal is to teach you how to work smart and not hard. There is no sense in you making the same mistakes that I have made. I am providing the following guide as a tool for you to learn from my past experience, save money, make and keep MORE of what you earn. One of my goals is to have a newsletter published each month that will help us all get to know one another, network, stay connected, and share tips and success stories. Let me know your thoughts and experiences and I will gladly share them with the group!

In this section you will learn the "nuts and bolts" of what it will really take to get you from "poverty to prosperity," in 90-days. We will explore a variety of strategies and techniques that you can use to build your real estate investment business. Should you decide to join our team, and become a Dollar-a-Day Real Estate Investor this year, you will be in business for yourself, but not by yourself. If two heads are better than one, imagine what a hundred or thousand could do!

There is enough business and money for everyone to become successful. This business was not created to help some people at the expense of others. It is my intent that anyone that comes in contact with this company through any of our team members should be blessed in more ways than just their financial bank accounts. I hope to attract thousands of like-minded people that are interested in not only improving themselves this year, but just as interested in joining a company where it's just as important if not MORE to focus on helping one another succeed!

Incentives: I would like your input to tell me specifically what you would like to experience as a valuable member of this company. Throughout the years it is common to hear people say what they would do if they were the boss, or if they were this or that…today is your chance to let your voice be heard and help create a company and environment with your own

Ideas might include training or mentorship opportunities through conference calls, workshops, seminars, or one-on-one. Group discounts for training and development resources, insurance, or special events. What type of prizes would you like to see offered as incentives? Cruises or vacation trips to exotic destinations, something a little less dramatic, like Disney World excursion for your family, or would you prefer more tangible personal items such as diamonds, cars, or gift cards? It's totally up to you. I say the next sentence, a little tongue in check, "Just like elections, if you don't let your voice be heard, don't complain about what you get in return!" ☺

It has been suggested is that we could offer weekly, monthly, or semi-monthly conference calls, and have the sessions available for download online for those that are interested. We could offer friendly competitions between teams in each city, region, or state each quarter and offer cash bonuses or other incentives to promote achievement and recognition on a regular basis.

I can easily see us having mini-conferences and celebration parties in each region, and holding one large conference each year for Dollar-a-Day Real Estate Investors. We could publish an annual Who's Who Yearbook as a way to showcase our members and their success stories.

☑ To Do Check Lists

Each week, you will receive a short training module and to-do list via email on a variety of topics that is designed to help you succeed as a Dollar-a-Day Real Estate Investor.

❏Sign Up - Registration Procedure

❏Determine Your Financial Objectives

❏Review & Determine What Strategies You Will Use

❏Create Your Strategic Plan
    Weekly / Monthly / 90-day Plan

❏Accountability Reporting

❏Order Magnetic Signs

❏Order Promotional Products

❏Begin Referral Partnership Development

❏Direct Mail Campaign

❏Coop Advertising

❏Affiliate Marketing

❏Email Auto responders, & Signatures

❏Website landing page

❏Twitter & Facebook Campaigns

☑ Sign Up Procedures

How to Join

To participate in any of our programs and become a Dollar-a-Day Real Estate Investor, you must be of sound mind and legal age. In the United States, that would be at least 18 years of age. Read, complete, sign, and return by email the Membership Application and Statement of Understanding that can be found in the appendix at the back of this book. This outlines the details and expectations for acceptance into the investor network.

Directions

To register as an Associate, Investor, or Affiliate, go to the Investor network website: www.iTrainInvestors.com. Your application will be processed immediately upon receipt.

Program-1- Lender Network:

In addition to the Membership Application, please fill out page 1 of the Promissory Note. Upon receipt of this application and promissory note, I will fill out my part of the loan agreement, sign, date, and email it back to you for your records. * A minimum investment of $30 per month, $500 total is required to participate in program as a Dollar-a-Day Real Estate Investor:

No income or credit restrictions to participate.
Level 1: $30 per month
Level 2: $50 per month
Level 3: $100 per month

☑ Laying the Foundation

❏ Overview

I have included an overview below for you to understand the Dollar-a-Day Real Estate Investment Wealth Building System.

Go back to Chapter 1 and review the financial objectives that you wrote for the upcoming year. Use the worksheets on the following pages to create your annual, quarterly, monthly, and weekly goals.

Once this is done, review which strategies are recommended for each type of goal that you have set, and determine what strategies you will use for the upcoming 90-days.

Your next step will be to create a 90-day, monthly, weekly, and daily plan to accomplish your goals. You will be required to submit your action plan as part of our accountability process. This short summary report is due by email no later than Saturday 5pm for the upcoming week.

Having an accountability partner has been proven to improve results. Although everyone involved will have different set of financial goals that they are trying to achieve, a fair way to compare results across the board will be to report the results based on the number of goals set, compared to whether the goal was achieved, rather than the specific dollar amount tied to the goal. Individual and team results will be posted each week. Financial incentives are available for achieving both personal, team, and company goals.

❏ Determine Your Financial Objectives

Directions: List each of your financial objectives, and use the recommendations in chapter one to identify which specific strategy is best suited and recommended for each specific type of financial goal. Circle the strategy(ies) available for each financial objective.

Count how many times you have circled each of the strategies, and write your answers in the blanks below the chart. This will help you decide which Dollar-a-Day Real Estate Investment strategies you must learn and implement to attain your financial goals this year.

We will use this information to help you create a personalized investment plan on the next few pages.

Objectives & Strategy

1. 123
2. 123
3. 123
4. 123
5. 123
6. 123
7. 123
8. 123
9. 123
10. 123

Strategy 1: _____
Strategy 2: _____
Strategy 3: _____

Calculating Financial Goals:

To help you achieve your goals, it is imperative that you break down each of your financial goals into an <u>annual, quarterly, monthly, and weekly goal.</u> Many people make mistakes calculating these numbers, especially when it pertains to their paychecks. They do not realize they could be losing hundreds or thousands of dollars each year by this one mistake. I have included the calculations and most common errors below.

This exercise will help you to set your financial goals for the upcoming 90-days. You can use these formulas to create your budget by inputting your monthly expenses into the same formulas.

Don't assume you know how to make these calculations correctly. Review the formulas below and check your own paystub to make sure you are getting paid what you think you are getting paid.

Monthly = 12 paydays per year
> Get paid one time per month

Weekly = 52 paydays per year
> Get paid each week

Bi-weekly = 26 paydays per year
52 weeks per year/2 = 26
> Get paid every other week

Semi-monthly = 24 paydays per year   12 months per year * 2 = 24
> Get paid two times per month, typically 1st and 15th of each month

Problem 1: $400 per week

Calculate annual and monthly, bi-weekly, semi-monthly paychecks

Annual Amount : Weekly amount X 52 weeks per year =
> 400 x 52 = $20,800 per year

Monthly Amount: Weekly amount X 52 weeks per year = Annual Amount / 12 months per year
$400 x 52= $20,800 $20,800/12 = $1,733.33 per month

Bi-weekly:
Annual amount / 26 $20,800 / 26= $800 every other week

Semi-monthly:
Annual amount / 24 $20,800 / 24= $866.67 two times per month

Problem 2:   **$3,700 per month**

Calculate annual, monthly, weekly, bi-weekly, semi-monthly paychecks

Annual: Monthly X 12 $3,700 x 12 = $44,400 per year

Weekly: Monthly x 12/52 $44,400 per year / 52 = $853.85 per week

Bi-weekly: Annual / 26 $44,400 / 26 = $1,707.69 every other week

Semi-monthly: annual / 24 $44,400 / 24 = $1,850.00 two times per month-

** Most Common Errors **:
Using problem 1, $400 per week, people mistakenly try to calculate the monthly amount by taking the weekly amount ($400) and multiply it by 4....incorrectly agreeing to **$1,600 per month**. As you can see from the correct calculation above, the monthly amount equivalent would be $1,733.33. If you are not careful, you could be losing $133.33 per month, or $1,599.96 per year!

The other error is not understanding the difference between bi-weekly and semi-monthly. Bi-weekly paydays are every other week, 26 paydays per year; Semi-monthly is 24 paydays per year. BE CAREFUL! Your paydays could be costing you money!

❏ Financial Goal Sheets   Annual / Monthly /Weekly / 90-day Plan

Complete the worksheet below to determine how much money you want to earn for each of your goals. Total each column at the bottom to get a grand total to use for your strategic planner worksheets.

Amount	Annual	Monthly	Weekly
1.			
2.			
3.			
4.			
5.			
6.			
7.			
8.			
9.			
Totals: $_____	Annual: $_____	Monthly: $_____	Weekly: $_____

How Much Real Estate Do I Need?

You might be interested in becoming a real estate investor in the traditional sense, meaning that one of your goals may be to purchase investment property with the money that you earn as a Dollar-a-Day Real Estate Investor.

Approximately how much real estate will you need to purchase to provide you with enough income each month to live, or to give you enough money to make a car payment, house payment, vacation, etcetera?

I have included a few examples to get you started. Each example is approximate, based on 20 years, and receiving a 5% return on your investment. Keep in mind that you may not need to come up with the full value of the real estate to purchase your properties. Once we gain enough participants in our network, you could use the power of the Dollar-a-Day Real Estate Investor Network to help finance your purchases. How?

Use your earned income to make the down payment, make a request to borrow the remainder from investors in the network to finance your properties, and use the rental income generated each month to pay the insurance, tax, your debt to the network, and any other expenses. Once the debt has been paid, the rental income generated is all yours!

To give you an idea of the possibilities, consider the following scenario: You find an excellent rental property that is worth much more than the $100,000 asking price. You work the numbers and do your market research to find out how much you can rent this property for, and realize this could be a great deal. You use your own money and put down 20%, or $20,000 and finance the remaining 80%, $80,000 through the network. You have just purchased a $100,000+ property for only a fraction of the cost, and your renters will pay off your debt! How many times can you do this? As many times as you like, there is no limit! A good deal, is a good deal.

You can purchase a fixed rate mortgage payment table book at any book store for around $7.95. I keep one with me at all times.

Real Estate Value
$500 per month/$6000 per year
$75,000

$1,000 per month/$12,000 per year
$155,000

$2,000 per month/$24,000 per year
$310,000

$5,000 per month/$60,000 per year
$750,000

For example, if you needed to generate about $500 per month, you could purchase $75,000 worth of real estate based on a 5% return. This is only a rough estimate to give you an idea of how much you would need, and does not factor in taxes, insurance, etcetera.

❏Create 90-day Financial Plan

Take the Monthly TOTALS from the previous page, multiply by 3, then divide by 12 to calculate your 90-day financial target amounts. Total each column at the bottom as in the worksheet on the previous page.

Monthly X 3 =	90-day Target /12=	Weekly Target for 90-days
1.		
2.		
3.		
4.		
5.		
6.		
7.		
8.		
9.		

Totals: Monthly: $_____ X 3 = 90-days $_____ /12= Weekly: $_____

❏Create 90-day Sales & Referral Partner Plan

By working "smart," and not "hard," leveraging yourself through the use of Referral Partners, or asking and receiving a minimum of 3 Referrals from EACH customer, you can easily achieve your financial target over the course of the next 90-days.

Use $10 commission to see how much you will have to produce working alone.

Use the $6 commission formula if you intend to enlist the help of Referral Partners. You will earn a $10 commission for each person that joins the network. Using Referral Partners, the commission split is a 60/40% split, or $6 and $4 respectively, with you earning $6, and your Referral Partner earning $4 each. You can show your referral partner the same formula to help them reach their own financial targets, just divide by $4, instead of $6.

Calculate using both of the formulas to see for yourself how powerful leveraging yourself and using referral partnerships to help you attain your financial goals. I have included a section in this chapter titled, "Show Me the Money," that shows you just how powerful asking for 3 referrals can be over the course of 90-days. I have included an example on the following page.

Referral Partner Worksheet

Income Goal for 90-days: $30,000
$30,000/$10 commission = **3,000 sales** required if you work by yourself

$30,000/$6 commission = *1-3 personal sales,* **5,000 total sales** required if you enlist the help of others
- To avoid fractions, each of the numbers has been rounded UP to the next whole number.

Sales Required: 5,000

Day 8
5000/3 = 1,667

Day 7
1667/3 = 556

Day 6
556/3 = 186

Day 5
186/3 = 62

Day 4
62/3 = 21

Day 3
21/3 = 7

Day 2
7/3 = 3

Day 1
3/3 = 1

How to interpret this information:

Your goal is to earn $30,000 over the course of the next 90-days or sooner, which equates to $10,000 per month or better. You decide to make a strategic plan and enlist the help of others to leverage yourself and your efforts to achieve your financial goals.

You may be astonished to realize that you could just as easily earn $30,000 in only 8 days if you follow the plan. This is not rocket science, or illegal, it's simply the same principle that explains the miracle of compound interest!

Example: If you were to put $1,000 in an interest bearing account that earns 10% per year on the day that your child is born, and never make any more deposits or withdrawals, when your child reaches retirement age, your $1,000 investment would have grown to a whopping 1 MILLION dollars thanks to the miracle of compounding interest!

How does it work? You started out with only a small $1,000 deposit, and at the end of the first year, you earned $100 in interest. The following year, you start out with $1,100 (1,000 + 100), earning 10% interest, (110), and so on and so forth until eventually your account balance over time has grown to one million dollars!

Earn 30,000 or more in 8-days

You find at least ONE person that desires to increase their income over the course of the next 90-days. Use this same worksheet to demonstrate how fast and easy it can be to reach their financial goals by following this same system. "Find at least 3 people that are interested in increasing their income over the next 90-days, and ask them to do the same."

The example above shows you how to generate more than $30,000 by starting with just ONE referral partner, and ask them to refer 3 people, and continue for 8 cycles. These cycles could be minutes, hours, days, weeks, or months depending on how you want to handle your referrals.

Personally, if given a choice, I would prefer minutes or days, which could easily occur if your referral partner used his email address contacts or social networks such as facebook or twitter to forward a simple invitation to join our network.

The financial possibilities are mind boggling if you hold each new member accountable and ensure they refer at least 3 people. This is just as beneficial to them as it is to you, as they earn a referral fee, and basically can get their membership for FREE just by referring a few people to join the network!

Imagine what would happen if you started with more than ONE referral partner? What if you could find one new referral partner each week for the entire 12 week period and had each of them doing the same? To see how many sales could be possible over the course of a 12 week period with just one referral partner, go to the chapter titled, "Show Me the Money."

But wait…there's MORE!

Keep in mind that this only pertains to the direct commissions that you earn, and does not include any royalty payments, business builder bonuses, or profit sharing bonuses from real estate investment activity inside the network!

1 Referral Partner			Earnings - 1 RP		
Day	Referrals	YR to Date	$6		$4
1	1	1	$ 6	$	4
2	3	4	$ 24	$	16
3	9	13	$ 78	$	52
4	27	40	$ 240	$	160
5	81	121	$ 726	$	484
6	243	364	$ 2,184	$	1,456
7	729	1,093	$ 6,558	$	4,372
8	2,187	3,280	$ 19,680	$	13,120
9	6,561	9,841	$ 59,046	$	39,364
10	19,683	29,524	$ 177,144	$	118,096
11	59,049	88,573	$ 531,438	$	354,292
12	177,147	265,720	$ 1,594,320	$	1,062,880
13	531,441	797,161	$ 4,782,966	$	3,188,644
14	1,594,323	2,391,484	$ 14,348,904	$	9,565,936

How to read this chart:

If you would like to earn $59,046, sign up 1 referral partner, and have them to refer at least 3 people, and teach them how to repeat the process. Have each referral partner **commit** to having this completed within a 24 hour period, and you will have earned $59,046 in 9 days! Your referral partner will have earned $39,394! Not a bad payday for 9 days of work, do you agree?

1 RP	2 RP	3 RP	4 RP	5 RP
$6	$6	$6	$6	$6
$ 6	12	18	24	30
$ 24	48	72	96	120
$ 78	156	234	312	390
$ 240	480	720	960	1,200
$ 726	1,452	2,178	2,904	3,630
$ 2,184	4,368	6,552	8,736	10,920
$ 6,558	13,116	19,674	26,232	32,790
$ 19,680	39,360	59,040	78,720	98,400
$ 59,046	118,092	177,138	236,184	295,230
$ 177,144	354,288	531,432	708,576	885,720
$ 531,438	1,062,876	1,594,314	2,125,752	2,657,190
$ 1,594,320	3,188,640	4,782,960	6,377,280	7,971,600
$ 4,782,966	9,565,932	14,348,898	19,131,864	23,914,830
$ 14,348,904	28,697,808	43,046,712	57,395,616	71,744,520

Would you like to earn that money quicker than 9 days or would you like to earn more than that? Instead of enlisting the help of only 1 Referral Partner, how about enlisting the help of 2, 3, 4, or 5? Look at the difference in your pay over the course of the same 9 days!

1 Referral partner $ 59,046
2 Referral Partners $ 118,092
3 Referral Partners $ 177,138
4 Referral Partners $ 236,184
5 Referral Partners $ 295,230

Referral Partner Worksheet

$_____/$10 commission = _____sales required

$_____/$6 commission = _____sales required

$_____/$4 commission = _____sales required

Sales Required: _____
2 week / 14 day cycle

1. _____/3

2. _____/3

3. _____/3

4. _____/3

5. _____/3

6. _____/3

7. _____/3

8. _____/3

9. _____/3

10. _____/3

11. _____/3

12. _____/3

13. _____/3

14. _____ = # of Referral Partners Required _____

Note:

Which do you think is easier? Attempting to obtain sales by yourself, or enlisting the help of others? The number of Referral Partners required assumes each sale or referral partner will provide the minimum 3 Referrals each, as stated in the Membership Agreement.

❐ Accountability

Every year people get excited and establish their New Year's resolutions, only to let them fall by the way side a month, week, or sometimes only mere days after they have made the commitment. Why do you think this happens? I don't think it's lack of willpower, I think it's a lack of accountability, or lack of enough positive influence that prevent us from follow through.

What happens if you tell someone you are going to do something and then don't follow through? It's embarrassing when they ask you about it, and eventually, you will develop a bad reputation for no follow through, yes? Have you ever decided to start exercising, or go to the gym, only to find yourself paying for a membership that is not getting used? Always something you have to do instead of go to the gym, am I right?

What if instead, you have a friend, and each of you are committed and promised one another to be a faithful workout partner, will meet at the gym 3 times a week, or go walking every morning at 7am? Which person do you think will be most successful? Research indicates the person with the accountability partner will be more successful because they don't want to let their partner down, and help one another stay focused and on task.

The same process will be used to help you achieve your financial objectives. At the beginning of your 12-week, 90-day cycle, you will be expected to establish your financial goals, set weekly targets, and email a weekly summary. Each week I will report the goals and results for the Company, Division, Region, District, and Team.

It will pay you huge financial dividends if you help your Referral Partners stay on track to reach their financial targets. One sure way is to have everyone commit to completing their 3 referrals within 24 hours. Show them the numbers. Procrastination doesn't pay. If they are able to refer 3 people within 24 hours, they can easily be on their way to earning big bucks within the week to 10 days!

Chapter 6:
Residual Money is Smart Money & How YOU Can Make It

Understanding residual or passive income

Residual income (also called passive or recurring income) is income that continues to be generated after the initial effort has been expended. Compare this to what most people focus on earning: linear income, which is "one-shot" compensation or payment in the form of a fee, wage, commission or salary.

Linear income is directly proportional to the number of hours invested in it (40 hrs. of pay for 40 hrs. of work), but one of the great advantages of residual income is that once things are set in motion, you continue making money from your initial efforts, while gaining time to devote to other things... such as generating more streams of residual income!

Examples of ways residual income can be earned:

1) Transfer the rights to a book you wrote, a software program you created, a gadget you invented, or a song you recorded, to a company that agrees to pay you a percentage of each copy of your work sold in the future.

2) Become an actor and draw residual income from each of your movies, TV shows, or commercials, each time they run.

3) Purchase real estate that earns you recurring income through lease or rental payment

4) Start a savings and investment program that pays you residual income in the form of interest or dividends.

5) Join associate programs. Call them what you will: referral, reseller, affiliate, bounty or associate programs, they are very popular on the Internet. Some of them offer similar opportunities for earning residual income.

Companies arrange such programs to compensate reps, resellers, dealers, associates, affiliates (or whatever the designation used) for promoting their products and services.

Reps are generally given a unique I.D. number and/or web page or site, so the company can track the source of each sale and compensate the proper rep.

Keep in mind that many associate programs only pay one-shot commissions, rather than recurring, residual compensation for your efforts.

Create a stream of residual income that will replace your current paycheck(s), improve the quality of your life and create a lifestyle that most can only dream about.

As I've shared with you previously...I'm not against earning some good, honest, "one-shot" linear income, but given a choice, which would *you* rather do: work hard and get paid only once, through linear income, or get paid continuously - perhaps for years or even the rest of your life - for hard work you perform only once, through residual income?

The Dollar-a-Day Real Estate Investment Company focuses on 3 types of residual income generating strategies, numbers 1, 3, and 5 above:

- Book Royalties
- Real Estate Investments
- Affiliate Programs

Chapter 7:
Rules, Regulations, & Suggestions

Although the rules are changing almost daily regarding solicitation, here are a few quick good rules of thumb and tips:

- Telemarketing: Do NOT call anyone, or use telemarketing of any kind to promote the business. If you make a mistake, you will be fined and we all could be held liable if you were to call anyone on the do not call registry list.

- Door Hangers: We CAN use door hangers, but your county, city, neighborhood, or housing association may have regulations or city ordinances against it. Better safe than sorry, so ASK to see if it's permissible in your area. Ignorance is no excuse. If you are considering using door-to-door marketing materials, make sure you are authorized to do so.

- Door-to-Door: Under NO circumstances should you knock on someone's door and solicit their business. This is unsafe as well as annoying to the other party.

- Parking Lots: Check with local authorities before you put out any flyers or post-it notes on people's cars or windows.

- Referral Partners: Check with you <u>local pizza or restaurant delivery</u> people to see if you can put our ad message on post-it notes, have the delivery drivers put the ads on their boxes and offer them a cut of your commission! <u>www.vistaprint.com</u> has 3x3 pads of 50 each with our logo included beginning at just $2.49 for 1 pad of 50, on up depending on the quantity you want to order. Order 5 pads of 50, (250 post it notes) for $7.49. You can Google "post it notes printing," and find other companies that can do it and get their pricing.

- Email & SPAM: Do not use unauthorized email blasts to send out spam messages. YES, you CAN use your contact lists of friends and family to help you successfully get the word out, and even use the auto responder signature on outgoing emails. The authorities are cracking down on people who are sending out unsolicited messages. I hate getting spammed, don't you? It's annoying, doesn't help us project the right image, and is against the law. Don't do it!

- On-line Social Media: YES, by all means you can use Facebook, Twitter, Blogs or other similar social media to promote your business. Keep in mind that you can't make any financial claims whatsoever, and to use only authorized wording. There are a few good books out there on this subject. I have begun to explore these options. I have been successful in getting quite a bit of coverage on the Google search engine. More news will follow as I report to you my findings. Email me and let me know how this is working for you!

- Affiliate Programs: Most of you may have heard about affiliate marketing programs offered via the internet, such as Google ad sense, amazon.com, and most any company these days that has a huge internet following. Basically you can put a referral link on your website, blog, or page, and depending on which program you are affiliated, if someone clicks on it and makes a purchase, they pay you a commission as a thank you for the referral. The other side of the coin is that we can advertise our company, and based on our budget, pay per click for people that click on our ad to learn more about the Dollar-a-Day Real Estate Investment Program. People are making a ton of money through affiliate marketing programs. Feel free to use this medium to your advantage.

- I am currently working on an Affiliate Program for this company. Once I get it up and running, I will post the information on the www.iTrainInvestors.com website. The way this will work is that Affiliates will sign up, and copy and paste a hyperlink on their blogs, websites, emails, twitter, facebook or other social networking forums. The program will track each visitor that clicks on a Dollar-a-Day Real Estate Investor advertisement or promotion. Every time someone purchases a product or joins the network, the Affiliate will earn a commission. The program provides great reporting tools so that we can easily identify what is working and what is not working.

Chapter 8:
Where's Your Sign?

A business with no sign, is a sign of no business! There is <u>NO requirement</u> for you to advertise or purchase promotional products for your business, but I do have them available should you decide this is something you wish to pursue. I have included some affordable options, tips and techniques you might want to consider to help you build your business.

How do people know you are in business? One of the most cost effective ways to get the word out quickly is by putting a <u>magnetic sign on your car</u>. People constantly come up to me and ask me about the sign on my car door. I always try to keep my car clean, and carry business cards and referral postcards in my purse just in case.

Look for High Traffic Areas

If you are a Referral Partner that lives or works in a high traffic or high visibility area, you may have to do nothing else but put a magnetic sign on your car door to make money! If you work at a retail establishment such as a dollar store, convenience store, or grocery store, you may easily have 500 or more customers a day within eye sight of your car. Think of it as a billboard sign that is working 24 hours a day! Imagine how powerful it would be if we had one or more cars sitting in every parking lot of a major retailer all across America advertising the Dollar-a-Day Real Estate Investor Network!

Make sure you do not solicit customers while you are working. Most employers have rules and regulations against this anyways, but even if they don't, please don't do it. When you are at work, give your employer the 100% commitment that they deserve.

Although we have a catchy website name, www.iTrainInvestors.com, it PAYS to be prepared, so always carry promotional tools or Referral Cards with you wherever you go. By the time a potential prospect gets back home, or to a computer, they might have forgotten the website name, or forgotten about what they saw...but if they have your <u>Referral Card,</u> they can get right down to business and check us out!

Promote Your Business: You have the option to purchase referral cards or any of our promotional products at wholesale cost. We take orders each month, purchase in bulk, and pass the savings along to you.

How to Order:

The information that I have provided below is quoted as of the date that I submitted this manuscript. Use this as a guide to give you an idea of pricing you can expect to pay for promotional items. You can also go online and get quotes. Please email for current pricing and minimum order quantities. I have included samples of direct mail postcards, referral cards, and logos for your perusal.

Go to the website www.iTrainInvestors.com to view the latest promotional products available. Feel free to email me suggestions on what you would like to see, and I will obtain a quote and post it on the website to see if there is any interest from others in the network to order so that we can save money by ordering in bulk.

Magnetic Signs for Your Automobile

I get my magnetic door signs from www.FastSigns.com. They are inexpensive, high quality, and offer a quick turnaround time. Typically once I submit my order, they are done by the next afternoon. Last time I purchased a set, I paid **$36.24** for two signs, one for each door.

This could be the least expensive, most important thing you could do to become a high earner. Imagine the possibility that you could easily double your current salary just by simply putting a sign on your car doors every day that you go to work or drive up and down the highway!. Always try to park your car in a high visible place where it will be seen by the most traffic. These signs easily come on and off, so you can choose when and where you use them to maximize your results.

For best results, I would suggest that you have them match the paint on your car for the words, but keep the dollar logo intact please. They can do this several ways, but I just drove my car up there, they pulled out their color swatches just like the strips you see at Home Depot, Lowes, or Wal-mart, and they match the color to your car.

Email me to request the artwork for the magnetic door signs. I get a ton of emails daily, so please put the words, "Magnetic Sign Request," in the subject line.

Postcards: .15 each

Minimum Order Quantity: 100
$15, plus postage for first class snail mail

Business Cards: .08 each

Minimum Quantity: 100
$8, plus postage for first class snail mail

Postcards and Business cards are double sided, full color, with shiny gloss finish. To view the current business cards and postcards that are authorized for use, go to www.iTrainInvestors.com. I will have them posted and updated on a regular basis.

* *Let me know if you would like a faster shipping method, such as UPS or FedEx. You will only be billed exactly what I am billed for the shipping or postage with no hidden charges or fees.

Advertising & Promotion

Nationwide Advertising & Promotion

Fifteen percent of the Network Management Fee that you pay each month goes towards a nationwide advertising and promotional ad campaign both offline and on-line. This campaign is designed to help you get your business off the ground, and start earning money by introducing *Dollar-a-Day Real Estate Investments* to people world-wide. Commissions generated will be divided equitably among all Program 2 Referral Partners and paid on the 1st and 15th of each month.

Coop Advertising

Coop Advertising is strictly <u>optional </u>but is available to you beginning with a minimum investment of $10 per month. You can increase this to any amount, depending on your budget for the month. How this works is that whoever wishes to participate in any given month will send me their advertising budget amount for the upcoming month by email, no later than <u>the 25th</u> of each month.

This gives me the opportunity to know how much we have to spend for the upcoming month and I can plan a specific ad campaign for the coop. For example, we might target cosmetologists, real estate agents, or certain newspaper or magazine publications. I then am able to negotiate and purchase ad space or whatever I need to conduct this particular ad campaign.

Coop Advertising fees are due to me <u>no later than the 1st</u> of each month so that I have time to order, receive, and begin work on the campaign the first week of the month.

Any profits from sales generated from the ad campaign will be distributed equitably to each participant based on their contributions. For example, if you contributed $10, and the coop had $100 to spend, your portion would be 10%, calculated as $10/$100.

Commissions earned from coop advertising will be sent electronically once a week.

Chapter 9:
Referral Partners

How to earn a considerable amount of cash in a short period of time

Referral Partnerships

Every investor that joins the network and participates in Program 2 is considered a Dollar-a-Day Real Estate Investment Company Referral Partner. You are paid to refer others to use our products and services. If you are interested in earning a considerable amount of money in a short period of time, you should really consider building a team of Referral Partners to help you achieve your financial goals in record time.

Not only will you be able to reach your financial goals in record time, but you will also be eligible to earn Bonuses based on the results of the team that you build.

If you have a lofty financial goal that you would like to reach within the next 90-days, working by the hour or using your individual efforts might not prove possible for you to reach your goals. However, by leveraging yourself through the use of Referral Partners, and teaching each of your Referral Partners how to duplicate what you are doing so that THEY can reach their financial goals, you can easily reach your financial goals by the allotted time frame!

If you would like to earn an insane amount of money over the course of the next 90-days, you should strive to create Referral Partnerships with people who have ACCESS TO lots of people on a daily or weekly basis.

I have shown you the financial power of starting with just one Referral Partner, asking them to refer 3, and continue the cycle. Imagine what would happen if instead, you had a TEAM of Referral Partners that had access to a

30 or more potential prospects each day? How quick do you think that you could reach your financial destination? Your income would grow exponentially over the course of 90-days, and it is entirely possible if you choose the right Referral Partners.

Who Might be the Perfect Referral Partner?

- Anyone who has a vehicle that works at a high traffic, high visibility place of business where the parking lot is always full of customers going in and out!
- Anyone who has a vehicle and travels a lot up and down the highway.
- Individuals who have a large circle of social capital and influence. Those that have a lot of friends, family members, community connections, on-line networks, etcetera
- Military families from all branches, stationed all over the world
- Licensed Cosmetologists, Barbers, Nail Techs, or Salon Owners
- Retailers or Service oriented businesses (think convenience stores)
- Pizza Delivery persons
- Real Estate Agents or similar professions

Referral Partnership Techniques for Success

The easiest people to contact would be your warm market; your family, friends, neighbors, co-workers, those people that you already have an established, positive relationship. However, for some of you, you may feel more comfortable exploring other options to gain referrals for your business. Feel free to use any technique that you feel most comfortable.

People who prefer no people contact whatsoever, might consider mailing out postcards to prospects in their community or to their target market. Others might prefer to use email, or social networking sites to gain Referral Partnerships.

Thousandaire, Millionaire, or Multi-millionaire?

Remember it's a numbers game. Don't take a rejection personally. The more people you ask to join your team, the closer you are to getting a YES. As you have seen in the referral partnership charts, it only takes 1 dedicated Referral Partner to help you earn a significant amount of cash in a short period of time. Gain 2 Referral Partners and you can easily become a Millionaire, Gain 3 or more and you are on your way to becoming a Multi-Millionaire! The choice is yours, which will it be?

With that said, you should hand out your referral cards to <u>everyone</u> you come in contact with; don't prejudge, or prequalify. We never know exactly who might be interested. Someone who might not have been interested a week or month ago, may be interested TODAY. It's a numbers game, and the greater the amount of people that know about us, the greater the likelihood of them joining your team. Put your referral card on all the bulletin boards in town where you can get permission.

I would suggest that you try to find people who work in high traffic locations, such as a convenience store, where they have several hundreds of customers coming in and out each and every day. Try to get one or more of their employees to become a Referral Partner and put one of the signs on their car, and get permission to set some business cards up by the cash register if at all possible.

I would then go to the hair and nail salons in your town. Stylists know everyone in town! Salons work on a typical 6 week cycle, which means their regular customers are on a schedule to get their hair done at least once every 6 weeks. If you want to make sure everyone in town knows about your business, it would be a safe bet to enlist the help of some of your friends down at the local beauty shop in town.

Some may not be willing to allow solicitation of their customers, but they could easily approve you to place Referral Cards at each work station and would be okay to allow their customers to request one. You would probably get the best response by asking the salon owner's permission to put them at the cash register, or ask the salon owner to become a Referral Partner and show her or him how they could reach their financial goals by enlisting the help of everyone in the salon. How many stylists work for the salon? How many customers do they see each day and week? This is a huge opportunity.

Imagine if the salon has 5 stylists and each of them work one customer every 15 minutes for a total of 4 per hour, 8 hours a day, 32 per stylist per day, 160 people per day per salon…would you like having access to 160 people per day? Do you think that any of those 160 people just might be interested in improving their bank accounts over the course of 90-days?

Cash Register Set-ups: Another option is to have the business cards or postcards set up by the cash register, bulletin boards, or where there is a lot of foot traffic. Every time someone pays for their merchandise or service, you can either drop a card in their bag, invite them to pick up a card, or just allow them to pick one up on their own accord. Imagine how many people visit convenience stores each day and week! Too easy!

Home Party Plan

Could you use an extra source of regular cash flow each week? Some of you may feel more comfortable working the program as a type of "Home Party Plan." You are probably familiar with the most popular home demonstration plans, such as Pampered Chef, Mary Kay Cosmetics, and Tupperware. Feel free to get creative.

The Basics

The basics of a home party plan is that you host a party, invite your friends over, demonstrate or give a short presentation of what you are offering, and allow them the opportunity to purchase what you are selling. You then ask those in attendance to book their own parties, encouraging them to do so by offering some sort of incentive, such as free or discounted merchandise, or referral fees.

By booking parties each week during your FREE time, you are building up your client base, your credibility, increasing your income, having fun, and making a difference in the lives of others!

There are a few variations in how we could possibly use the party plan as a way to promote the Dollar-a-Day Real Estate Investment Program, leveraging your time so that you become a top earner within a relatively short period of time. **Don't forget to check with your tax advisor to identify all the possible ways you can save on your tax bill by keeping track of all your business expenses, such as gas & mileage on your vehicle, office supplies, computer, printer, internet use, and cell phone, etcetera.

1. You could invite a few people over to your house each week or month, or ever how often you feel comfortable, and have a presentation and question and answer session. You could have books available to sell, along with sign-up sheets, and internet access to sign people up on the spot. Short, sweet, to the point... plan on 1 hour max.

2. Encourage others to host a Real Estate Investment Party for you. You would travel to their home, present the program, sign people up, and repeat...repeat...repeat.

3. Leverage yourself by training others duplicate your system and to do the same! Everyone makes money and it becomes a win-win for everyone involved!

Run the numbers…how many parties would it take to increase your weekly income by $100, $250, or $1,000 per week?

If you are interested in the Home Party Plan option, send me an email and I will create and provide you with a presentation template and coaching tips.

Chapter 10:
Show Me the Money

Goal: 10 Referral Partners

If you started today, and enlisted the help of 10 Referral Partners, and asked each of them to tell just 3 people each THIS WEEK, and that cycle continued for 12 weeks, (90-days). Multiple the total referrals column by $6, to see how much income is being generated each week.

Week	Referrals	Total Referrals
1	10	10
2	30	40
3	90	130
4	270	400
5	810	1,210
6	2,430	3,640
7	7,290	10,930
8	21,870	32,800
9	65,610	98,410
10	196,830	295,240
11	590,490	885,730
12	1,771,470	2,657,200

Week 1: At the end of week 1, you will have told 10 people about the program, for a total of 10 people.

Week 2: those 10 people have told 3 people each, for a total of 30 new people introduced, plus the original 10 people that you first introduced, total of 40 people now know about the Dollar-a-Day Real Estate Investment Company.

It starts getting exciting after week 3…by asking every person you know to help get the word out, your network can grow to an astonishing 2.6 MILLION people in just 12 short weeks by just starting out with only 10 people…but why stop there? Imagine how quick this could happen if you just sent out an email?

By continuing to introduce at least 10 people per week to the program, the word of mouth is growing exponentially to a staggering number! For every 10 people that you tell, look what could happen in only a 12 week period!

Keep in mind those people that might become excited about the real possibilities and tell every person they know! Just ONE excited person could really put you over the top!

Why is this important?

The more people that learn about our company, the more likely they are to purchase our products and/or join our network. Every time they do, YOU GET PAID! For every person that joins our network thanks to YOUR referral efforts, you earn $10 each, $6 if you use a referral partner…let's run a few numbers here:

Goal: $250 per week

of Referral Required: $250/$10 commission = 25 referrals required
25/3= 8 people……ask just 8 people to refer 3 people, OR ask 5 people to refer 5 of their friends, or ask 1 to refer 3, and have them do the same! Which is easiest?!

Learn to work "smart," and not "hard." Which is easiest? You beating the pavement trying to obtain 25 referrals on your own each week, or enlisting the help of others to help you achieve your goal?

This is an extremely easy task once you understand how to leverage yourself and enlist the help of others to help you get the word out! People are spending more on fast food, tanning, and getting their nails done than what they could be on joining our network and improving their personal finances! In today's economy, everyone is searching for ways to increase their income. Dollar-a-Day Real Estate Investments is a great bargain.

How much would you like to earn each week? $_____

Who should you ask? EVERYONE.

Team Share Bonuses: Keep in mind there are several ways in which you earn money. You earn a commission based on your individual efforts, and also as a Bonus based on the results of everyone in the company.

Chapter 11:
Niche Marketing & Territories

Our coop marketing plans will be based around niche marketing and specific targeted zip code areas. I encourage you to do the same. We don't want to be targeting the same groups of people because that would be a <u>waste of time, energy, and money.</u> I have included the primary targets below as a courtesy so that you are aware of where our coop marketing campaign dollars will be spent in the upcoming year.

- Retail Managers of top chains
- Licensed cosmetologists, nail techs, barbers, & salon owners
- Real Estate Agents
- Military Families
- Top Military Installations
- Military Newspapers
- Thrifty Nickel & Penny Pincher Classified Ads

Chapter 12:
Direct Mail Techniques

Although it cost almost nothing to refer in person, one option you might want to consider is direct mail, where you mail out our postcards to households or businesses across the nation. You are free to mail the approved referral postcards to anyone that you please. I do have a few recommendations based on my past experience that I think will prove helpful, will save you money, increase your response rates, and prevent direct mail headaches.

NO Bulk Mail

The first tip is do NOT use bulk mail to mail out your postcards. Although you will save money on the postage, what they don't tell you is that the bulk mail gets sit in a corner until they have a lull or slow period, then it goes out. Time is a precious commodity, and this process can take a very long time from start to finish. The other part of this equation is that any mail that is undeliverable will be thrown away, rather than returned to us...which is a very important tracking measurement.

Use First Class Mail

Use first class mail, it will arrive on time, in just a day or two, and if the address is bad, it will be returned to us so that we can clean up our database. Postcard rates are cheaper than regular letter rates, so if you choose this rate, you will be saving money anyways.

What Day Should I Mail?

Don't mail out during the busy times because your mail will be mixed in with all the other bills or junk in the mailbox. Watch your own mailbox for tips on when would be the best time to mail out in your neighborhoods. Obviously do not mail out in time for the receiver to get during the holidays, on the weekend, or the first and end of the month billing statement cycle times. If I had to choose a day of the week for mail to arrive to a prospect, it would be on Tuesday or Wednesday.

Always Include Yourself

I always address one postcard in each mail out to myself to gauge how long it takes from the date I drop it off to the post office to the date I get it delivered to my mailbox, and to determine what condition the postcard or mail piece arrives to my mailbox.

Returned Mail

My return address is on all the postcards, and I am able to track our response rate and identify problem areas almost immediately. I will contact you if and when I receive any back with bad addresses so that we have an accurate count of how much of our mail is actually deliverable as addressed.

Where to Get the Mailing List Addresses

You can use the phone book, the internet, or county tax assessor's records for FREE to get your addresses for a mail out. Some methods are more time consuming than others and depending on your time and budget, you may want to consider just purchasing a mailing list from a broker and downloading it to Microsoft Word, and printing out the labels. Your choice.

I have had great luck with www.infousa.com for purchasing my mailing lists. This is a reputable, well-known company that keeps its lists up to date and has a variety of options to suit whatever it is that you are trying to accomplish. No need to order all the fancy bells and whistles, you just need the name and mailing addresses. Once you pay for it, the file is sent to you and you can download and start using it immediately.

You can use this site for budget planning as well. Go on there and get the counts for a specific zip code, age group, household income, city, state or whatever target market you are considering. It is a great resource and tool for your marketing.

There may be a company out there that is cheaper, just make sure it is reputable. Info USA has been around for quite some time and is a leader in the industry. Again, track your response rates and how many are returned to see how good your list is. Keep in mind that people are moving all the time, and a little error is to be expected.

Response Rates:

It's important to track your response rate to see how well your direct mail efforts are paying off. You can calculate this by how much you spend, versus the commissions you earned from these efforts. Obviously the goal is to make more money than you spend...so read the tips!

Keep a Log

Make sure you are consistent and keep a detailed log on when and how you mail out your direct mail pieces. Just like in any advertising effort, it takes consistent effort, and several attempts before you get someone's attention.

Trial Run

I would suggest that you do a trial run of 100 postcards to see which one works the best. I would mail out 50 postcards, then I would mail out the other 50 inserted into an envelope, with a return address that includes my Name and address, and NOT the company name. Colored envelopes tend to work better, and handwritten envelopes (rather than computer labels) have worked better for me as well. You can purchase these envelopes at Wal-Mart or office supply store. Make sure that your postcards will fit inside...4x6.

It's more expensive but...

If you mail out just the postcard, you will only pay the postcard rate for postage. Now that we have an envelope involved, you will pay the regular postage for a letter. Yes, it's more expensive, because now you have to purchase the postage AND the envelope, but it's been my experience that people tend to pay more attention to the ones that I have sent in an envelope because it looks like an invitation and might be something important.

They might just toss the postcard. It's a roll of the dice either way. Just try it and see what you experience tells you. Every market is a little different, so yours may be different from someone else's. The goal is to get your response rates high enough so that you are generating enough sales to meet your financial objectives. Although it may cost you more, the higher response rate may indicate it's a better use of your budget to include the envelope. Let me know how it goes.

Don't Forget Your Referral Code

Make sure your referral information is included on the postcard so that you get credit for the referral. I have a space designated for your information on the front of each postcard. I would suggest that you use the Avery 8195 white return address label for this purpose. They are the perfect size 2/3 x 1 ¾", and come in an envelope of 600, which is 10 pages of labels, which have 60 on each page. You can purchase these online, your local office supply store, or Wal-Mart.

Classified Ads

We have to be extremely careful when advertising the Dollar-a-Day Real Estate Investment Program. Due to legal implications, it is imperative that we not confuse or mislead consumers in any way, shape, form or fashion. Be very clear and understand that we are not offering investment advice, securities, stocks, bonds, mutual funds, or anything of this nature.

Note
This is not a public offering. This is not an offer or invitation to sell or a solicitation of any offer to purchase any securities in the United States or any other jurisdiction. Any securities may only be offered or sold, directly or indirectly, in the state or states in which they have been registered or may be offered under an appropriate exemption.

When we are advertising, we are promoting the Dollar-a-Day Real Estate Investment Training Program, which teaches everyday people specific strategies that they can use to earn money to by joining forces with our company, the Dollar-a-Day Real Estate Investment Company. This program is currently available as a Microsoft Word e-book for download, and soon will be available as a paperback and hardback version from over 150,000 retailers online.

Authorized ads:

The following word and display ads are authorized for your use. I have included samples of direct mail & promotional items at the end of this section. Check online at www.iTrainInvestors.com for the latest authorized ads and marketing materials that are available.

Dollar-a-Day Real Estate Investments
Now available nationwide.
www.iTrainInvestors.com

Dollar-a-Day Real Estate Investments
Strategies for Everyday People
www.iTrainInvestors.com

You can use this AD for: Post-it notes for pizza delivery boxes, flyers, door hangers, frig magnets, or anything else that you can think of to promote your business!

Chapter 13:
Promotional Products

It is my job to provide you with the tools that you need to be successful. With that in mind, you are able to purchase any of the promotional products at wholesale cost, including books.

The image and standard that I wish to convey for the Dollar-a-Day Real Estate Investment Company is polished, professional, and high quality. I understand desktop publishing is available on most any laptop or desktop computer these days, but primarily due to the legalities involved,we must stay consistent as a team, and use the same tools for the branding, positioning, and promotion of our company, and its products and services.

If you find something that you like and think it would benefit everyone in the network to help us promote the business better, please send me an email, link, or sample and I will gladly check it out and get the consensus of the group.

I have included samples of direct mail and promotional items at the end of this section.

Bulk Orders = Savings for YOU

If I am able to order in large quantities, I can pass the savings on to you. This goes for business cards, postcards, brochures, frig magnets, signs, and most any type of promotional product. The more you purchase, the cheaper the price becomes.

Individually, it would be expensive and cost prohibitive to order high quality materials, for the low quantity that you probably would be using on a personal basis; however, collectively we can pool our resources and purchase items in bulk, enabling you to get a far superior product for less money. A win-win for everyone.

Summary

It has never been a better time to invest in real estate. The Dollar-a-Day Real Estate Investment Program offers you a variety of options and strategies to make the most of your money this year. You can choose one, or choose ALL options to help you achieve your financial dreams…for only a $1 per day, or $30 per month minimum investment!

Overview:

1. **Fixed rate of return**: Earn a fixed rate of return by serving as one of our private lenders. You will receive a promissory note backed by real estate as collateral.

2. **Earn cash fast:** Pay your bills or build your own real estate investment empire with the cold-hard cash earned through a variety of referral partner, affiliate marketing programs, and profit-sharing bonus plans. Participate in coop advertising to boost your commissions!

   This is a work-at-home business opportunity where you promote our products and services and receive a commission based on your individual efforts, and earn profit-sharing bonuses based on the efforts of everyone participating.

3. **Residual Income:** Earn cash quarterly through the royalty payments received from the sale of our books and publications.

To get started in any of these programs immediately, you can email nancy. gaskins@operationHSH.com and request a hard copy version of the application, and promissory note. Complete the application and submit for consideration.

I look forward to working with you and helping you achieve all your financial dreams this year!

To your financial success!

Nancy Gaskins, the
Dollar-a-Day Real Estate Investor

Example of a Flyer for a Seminar

Example of Meet the Author Poster

Just Published...

Live Like You Are Dying
How to Transform Your Life in 30 Days

Nancy Gaskins, MBA - Challenge-to-Succeed Academy
www.NancyGaskins.com

This guidebook provides the tools and inspiration to help everyone discover and achieve their true destiny, despite their past or current circumstances, in just thirty days.

iUniverse™   Call 1-800-AUTHORS to order, or visit www.iUniverse.com

Just Published...

Live Like You Are Dying
How to Transform Your Life in 30 Days

Nancy Gaskins, MBA - Challenge-to-Succeed Academy
www.NancyGaskins.com

This guidebook provides the tools and inspiration to help everyone discover and achieve their true destiny, despite their past or current circumstances, in just thirty days.

iUniverse™   Call 1-800-AUTHORS to order, or visit www.iUniverse.com

Example of Postcard to Announce the Publication

Examples of Bookmarks

Nancy Gaskins

Live Like You Are Dying

CMR 415 Box 4963
APO AE 09114
United States

phone 011490964560̄2782

Nancy.Gaskins@operationHSH.com

To Order, Call 1-800-AUTHORS, or visit www.iUniverse.com

Nancy Gaskins

Live Like You Are Dying

CMR 415 Box 4963
APO AE 09114
United States

phone 0114909645602782

Nancy.Gaskins@operationHSH.com

To Order, Call 1-800-AUTHORS, or visit www.iUniverse.com

Nancy Gaskins

Live Like You Are Dying

CMR 415 Box 4963
APO AE 09114
United States

phone 0114909645602782

Nancy.Gaskins@operationHSH.com

To Order, Call 1-800-AUTHORS, or visit www.iUniverse.com

Nancy Gaskins

Live Like You Are Dying

CMR 415 Box 4963
APO AE 09114
United States

phone 0114909645602782

Nancy.Gaskins@operationHSH.com

To Order, Call 1-800-AUTHORS, or visit www.iUniverse.com

Nancy Gaskins

Live Like You Are Dying

CMR 415 Box 4963
APO AE 09114
United States

phone 0114909645602782

Nancy.Gaskins@operationHSH.com

To Order, Call 1-800-AUTHORS, or visit www.iUniverse.com

Nancy Gaskins

Live Like You Are Dying

CMR 415 Box 4963
APO AE 09114
United States

phone 0114909645602782

Nancy.Gaskins@operationHSH.com

To Order, Call 1-800-AUTHORS, or visit www.iUniverse.com

Nancy Gaskins

Live Like You Are Dying

CMR 415 Box 4963
APO AE 09114
United States

phone 0114909645602782

Nancy.Gaskins@operationHSH.com

To Order, Call 1-800-AUTHORS, or visit www.iUniverse.com

Nancy Gaskins

Live Like You Are Dying

CMR 415 Box 4963
APO AE 09114
United States

phone 0114909645602782

Nancy.Gaskins@operationHSH.com

To Order, Call 1-800-AUTHORS, or visit www.iUniverse.com

Nancy Gaskins

Live Like You Are Dying

CMR 415 Box 4963
APO AE 09114
United States

phone 0114909645602782

Nancy.Gaskins@operationHSH.com

To Order, Call 1-800-AUTHORS, or visit www.iUniverse.com

Business Cards Promoting Books

201

Examples of Promotional Materials

To view the latest marketing and publicity materials in full color, visit the website www.iTrainInvestors.com.

Here you will find examples of postcards, business cards, flyers, brochures, magnetic car signs and other items that we have available for members to promote the Network.

Referral Cards – Business Cards

Example of magnetic sign for your car

Niche Marketing – Military Families

Part VII

Future Profiles of Success

Advertising Information

Directory

Directory Information

The Dollar-a-Day Real Estate Investment Company operates strictly from referrals. In order to join one of our investor networks, or purchase a product or service, you must include the referral source so that our Referral Partners earn credit for the referral. Feel free to browse the Investor Network Directory and contact any of our Investors to request a Referral.

This Directory will be updated on a quarterly basis. This book and book series, *"In Pursuit of the American Dream,"* is available worldwide at over 150,000+ retailers online, such as www.iUniverse.com, Barnes and Noble Booksellers, www.bn.com, Amazon, www.amazon.com, among others.

The names and contact information of Investors in the Dollar-a-Day Real Estate Investment Network will be published alphabetically, by Country, State, and City; then Last name, first Name. You can opt to just have your name listed, or name and contact information. A FREE listing in the online directory, which rotates on a continuous basis, is available for those that advertise in this directory. Introductory pricing is available for only $30 per quarter, ($10 per month,) is limited to 500, and will be on a first-come, first-serve basis.

Obtaining a listing in the directory is a great way for you to gain world-wide exposure and earn commissions from referrals, and advertise for potential investment partners to help fund your real estate investment purchases!

Submit your Directory Listing via email to:DirectoryListing@ operationHSH.com.

Sponsors

These pages are reserved for businesses or individuals that offer products and/or services that specifically support real estate investors. To become a sponsor, go to the website, www.iTrainInvestors.com, and register as a Sponsor, or email sponsor@operationHSH.com.

Platinum - $100 or more
> Display Ad – ½ page

Gold - $50
> Display Ad – ¼ page

Bronze - $25
> Display Ad – 1/8 page

Silver - $10
> Company Name & Contact Info Listing

Preferred Real Estate Agents

This space is reserved for licensed Real Estate Agents to advertise the fact that have experience with or are interested in working with the Dollar-a-Day Real Estate Investors. To become a Preferred Agent, email NewAgent@operationHSH.com. Introductory offer $50 for 12 months.

Corporate Contributors

This space is reserved for those businesses that directly contribute to the overall success of the Dollar a Day Real Estate Investors in our network by helping to offset the costs of Training and Development. Workshops, seminars, conferences, educational resources and materials, webinars, conference calls, newsletters, and other similar publications that help educate or promote the Dollar-a-Day Real Estate Investment Program.

Corporate Contributor: $250

- 1 page display ad in this publication
- Listing in all conference, workshop, and seminar materials.

Investor Network

STATE

Last Name, First Name
City, State, Zip
Website address (optional)
Email address (optional)
Telephone (optional)
Specialty: (Optional)

FLORIDA

Gaskins, Nancy
Destin, Florida 32550
www.iTrainInvestors.com
nancy.gaskins@operationHSH.com
(850) 499-7149
Specialty: Residential Real Estate,

Preferred Real Estate Agents

STATE

Last Name, First Name
Business Name
City, State, Zip
Website address (optional)
Email address (optional)
Telephone (optional)

Sponsors / Corporate Contributors

1 box = 1/8 page
2 boxes = ¼ page
4 boxes = ½ page
8 boxes = 1 page

APPENDIX

Application and Promissory Note
Bio & Contact Information
Recommended Books & Subject Matter
What's Next?

Bonus
Challenge to Succeed Strategic Planner Worksheets
Introducing the Master Plan for Life Management System

Application & Promissory Note

Dollar-a-Day Real Estate
Investor Network

Application – Page 1

You must be at least 18 years of age to participate in the Dollar-a-Day Real Estate Investor Network.

Name:

Date of Birth:

Current Age:

Social Security # or Tax ID # for Income Tax Reporting Purposes:

> ***Note:*** You will receive a 1099 at the end of the year for any commissions, royalty payments, or interest earned from the Dollar-a-Day Real Estate Investment Company. Check with your tax advisor, accountant, or go to www.irs.gov to learn more about the requirements of reporting income, and what type of expenses qualify as tax deductions for those that are self-employed.

Mailing Address:

Telephone:

Email:

Referred by:

Name:

Email:

Other Contact Information:

We operate strictly from referrals.
Your application will not be processed until your provide a referral source.

Statement of Understanding & Agreement - Page 2

As a Member of the Dollar-a-Day Real Estate Investor Network, you are eligible, but <u>not required</u> to participate in any of the investment network programs that are available. Visit the Network Website to view the current Membership Agreement, Promissory Note, and opportunities that are available for Dollar-a-Day Real Estate Investors. (**www.iTrainInvestors.com.**)

<u>No Guarantees</u>: As in any business, there are no guarantees of income expressed or implied by Nancy Gaskins or the Dollar-a-Day Real Estate Investment Company. The strategies outlined in the Dollar a Day Real Estate Investment Program are created in an effort to help everyday people earn enough money to afford to purchase real estate for cash, with no mortgage, in a short period of time.

Get Your Membership FREE: To help YOU get your Membership for FREE, to keep our overhead expenses low, and our administrative and management costs affordable, we ask that every applicant refer at LEAST 3 people to the Network. You will be paid a $10 commission for each referral. If you refer 4 people, you will have already paid for your annual membership and are making a profit by helping others improve their finances this year

Referral Name   **Email and Mailing Address**
1.
2.
3.
4.

Note

This is not a public offering. This is not an offer or invitation to sell or a solicitation of any offer to purchase any securities in the United States or any other jurisdiction. Any securities may only be offered or sold, directly or indirectly, in the state or states in which they have been registered or may be offered under an appropriate exemption.

<u>Marketing & Promotional Materials</u>: You are not required to purchase any advertising or promotional items, however, it is my intent to provide and make available to network members, top notch, professional, and polished advertising, marketing and promotional materials that adheres to any and all legal restrictions and guidelines, and something of which you can be proud.

If I order items such as business cards, brochures, postcards, book marks, and advertising in bulk quantities on a regular basis, we will able to save a tremendous amount of time and energy and I can pass the savings along to you. There is no sense in reinventing the wheel or possibly printing something or making a statement that could be misconstrued and potentially cause you, other network members, or the company to be held personally liable from a legal standpoint. We can also track the success or failure of each of the strategies used; make immediate corrections, simply by allowing you to make comments and suggestions each week on how things are working.

You can purchase these items direct from me, lower quantities, at wholesale cost, rather than retail, which is what you would pay if you went directly to a printer. You do have the option to use your own printing company, but I must approve the final product prior to distribution. This will ensure the quality and integrity of what you are distributing with our name attached.

Coop Advertising: You can participate in coop advertising each month with a minimum of $10 per month. Each week and/or month, depending on how much money is available in the coop, we will promote the company and products through direct mail and ad placements in newspapers, and online. Any commissions earned from sales generated from the coop will be distributed equitably based on the amount you contributed. For example, if the coop earned a total of $1000 in commissions, and your coop contribution percentage was 10% of the total invested, you would earn $100. Again, we can't guarantee that there will be sales, but by working together, we are able to pool our money and purchase more and better quality advertising in hopes of obtaining sales.

Payments – All payments to and from Dollar-a-Day Real Estate will be through www.paypal.com. Paypal accepts debit cards, credit cards, and electronic checks. Commission checks will be paid out daily upon receipt, until further notice. Team share bonus checks will be paid out on a quarterly basis, one week from the date of royalty payment disbursement from our publisher.

Statement of Understanding & Agreement - Page 3

How You Earn Commissions

Network Membership: $10 each

Every time someone joins the Dollar-a-Day Real Estate Investor Network and uses your name or referral code as the source, you will earn $10.

Referral Partners: 60%/40% split $6 / $4 each

Every time one of your Referral Partners generate a sale, you will earn a commission of $6, and they will earn $4.

Leadership Bonuses: 5% Payout

As an incentive to help you achieve your financial goals in a timely manner, you have the option to earn additional income each month in the form of a Bonus. To be eligible for leadership bonuses, you must build a team of Referral Partners. For example, once you have 5 Referral Partners working for you, you become a Manager, and are eligible to receive a Bonus each month based on the results of your team, in addition to any commissions!

Manager: 5 Referral Partners (5RPs)	2%
District Manager: 5 Managers (25 RPs)	1.5%
Regional Manager: 5 District Managers (125 RPs)	1%
Division Manager: 5 Regional Managers (725 RPs)	.5 %

Book Rep: You may purchase books at a 25% discount, and sell them at full retail. Paperback books typically retail for $15.95, and hardback $24.95. Minimum purchase of 10 books prepaid to qualify for bulk discounts. This is quite a bargain for a complete investment program!

Great for home party plan, workshops, seminars, conferences, job fairs, trade booths, or flea market booths!

Book sale: 60/40 split. If you refer someone to our website and they purchase a book direct from me, you will receive 40% of my commission earned upon receipt. Depending on the volume of orders I place each month, I am eligible to purchase my books from the publisher at a discount. No fancy formulas, you will get 40% of whatever profit I earn from the sale.

Sponsors/Corporate Contributors/Real Estate agents: You will receive a 10% commission for directory listings that we receive based on your efforts.

Royalty Payments: As a thank you courtesy, by joining and supporting the Dollar-a-Day Real Estate Investor Network, you are eligible to receive a portion of all royalty payments received from our book publisher(s) each quarter in the form of a team share bonus.

Online bookstores are open 24/7 around the world. I have no control over whom or when someone will purchase one of our books. However, every time someone does purchase one of our books from one of these 150,000+ online retailer websites, we will earn and receive a royalty check, and YOU will receive a cash BONUS, just for being part of our network!

Typically, we receive a 15-20% royalty payment on net proceeds from our publisher. Bookstore resellers purchase our books at wholesale from our publisher, and sell them at retail. Net proceeds refer to the amount that our publisher received less any returns.

As a thank you for participating, 10% of royalty payments received will be earmarked and distributed as <u>CASH bonuses</u> to each active member in the network, based on the number of referral credits they have earned.

- Network Member, 0 Referrals= .5 credits
- Book Sale Referral=1credit each
- Network Membership Referral=2 credits each

Example: $5,000 royalty payment received from publisher = $500 team share bonus available

For this example, we will assume 100 credits have been earned in the network during this quarter.

You personally earned 10 credits or 10% = 10/100=10%

Your bonus = $500 x 10% = $50.

Statement of Understanding & Agreement - Page 4

Network Directory: To help establish yourself as a Dollar-a-Day Real Estate Investor, earn Referral Commissions, and locate investors to help you fund your projects, you have the option to advertise your name and contact information in the Investor Directory located in the back of the Dollar-a-Day Real Estate Investments book for only $30 each quarter. You will receive a FREE listing on the On-line directory. This is a limited time offer, available only to the first 500 prepaid network investors. To gain world-wide recognition, and take advantage of the numerous opportunities and benefit as a real estate investor, a directory listing can help. Our book distribution channel contains over 150,000 retailers online!

Enrollment Fee: $35 per Year

Network Membership is valid for a 12 month period, beginning from the date we receive your membership application and payment. Fees will not be prorated.

As a Member of the Dollar-a-Day Real Estate Investor Network, you are eligible, but not required to participate in any of the investment network programs that are available.

Program 1: Fixed, rate of return with Promissory Note, minimum investment $500

Program 2: Work-at-Home Business Opportunity

> Earn Commissions & Bonuses based on sales of Dollar-a-Day Real Estate Investment Network Memberships, products, and services. $365 per year (includes Management Fee)
>
> Payment Plan: $1/day, $30 per month
>
> Purchase and maintain real estate investment properties and supporting assets. Advertise, promote, and manage the day to day operations of the Dollar-a-Day Real Estate Investment Company Network, products, and services.

Program 3: Residual Income Earning Opportunity
Any network member in good standing is eligible

_____Signature

_____Date

Dollar a Day Real Estate Investment Company

Promissory Note   Page 1

Program 2:   Referral Partnership Affiliates

Fee: $365   Includes 100 Referral Cards, World-wide Advertising &
Promotion, Management Fee, & option to advertise in the
Investor Directory.

VALUE RECEIVED from the Investor by the following payment method:
___ Lump Sum: $365 OR
___ $1 per day, $30 per month for 12 months
**No penalty for early payoffs

Purpose:
Purchase and maintain real estate investment properties and supporting assets.
Advertise, promote, and manage the day to day operations of the Dollar-a-Day
Real Estate Investment Company Network, products, and services.

Payments will begin: _____

Monthly payments are to be made electronically by www.paypal.com.

Investor will be billed monthly for their contribution payment.

Commission & Bonuses earned will be paid as stated in the Membership
Agreement.

_____

Investor Signature

Date:
___ (Initial to indicate your agreement)

Program 1: Fixed Rate of Return

Investors: I understand that my investment is a <u>loan</u> to be used to purchase and maintain real estate investment properties, promote, and manage the day to day operations of the Dollar-a-Day Real Estate Investment Company Network.

My loan will be paid back out of the net income generated from the investment properties purchased. I am free to sell, or assign my investment interest to others as stated in the membership rules and regulations.

I will be paid a fixed rate of return as specified in the promissory note.

___ (Initial to indicate your agreement)

I have read, understood, and agree to the rules and regulations regarding my Membership. As with any investment, I understand there may be inherent risks associated with this investment. I understand that all investment funds will be held in an interest bearing account until a real estate transaction has occurred. If for whatever reason, the real estate investment project is not able to be funded; my investment will be returned, along with any interest earned.

Date you wish your investment payment plan to begin: _____
(type in date)

Highlight your choices below in **BOLD**

___Weekly   ___Monthly   ___Semi-monthly (2X per month)

Saturday   1st of each mth 1st, & 15th

Amount per pay period above: $_____ *OR*

Lump sum to be paid on this date._____

_____Signature

_____**Date**

Dollar a Day Real Estate Investment Company

Promissory Note   Page 1

Program 1 Investors

Amount: $_____
(12 month period total, minimum $500)

VALUE RECEIVED from the Investor by the following payment method:
   $____ per month for ____months **OR**
   $____per month for ____months, plus lump sum payment of $____ OR
   _____ lump sum payment(s) of $_____

Purpose:
Purchase and maintain real estate investment properties and supporting assets, advertise, promote, and manage the day to day operations of the Dollar-a-Day Real Estate Investment Company Network.

Payments will begin: _____

Monthly payments are to be made electronically by www.paypal.com.

Investor will be billed monthly for their contribution payment.

_____

Investor Signature

Date:

Dollar a Day Real Estate Investment Company

Promissory Note   **Page 2**

Program 1: Fixed Rate of Return Investors

Date: _____

FOR VALUE RECEIVED, the undersigned, Nancy Gaskins DBA Dollar-a-Day Real Estate Investment Company, mailing address 10859 Emerald Coast Parkway, Ste. 204, #334 – Miramar Beach, Florida 32550 promises to pay to the order of:

Investor /Member Name:_____, at

Address: _____ or such other place as the holder may designate in writing to the undersigned, the principal sum of [$_____], together with interest thereon from date hereof until paid, at the rate of ___% **APR** - (___ percent annual percentage rate) per annum as follows:

Loan Re-Payment Options:
Quarterly Cash OUT – Each quarter, beginning 90-days from date of closing on each property.

Once the budgeted bills have been accounted for and paid, a minimum of 40% of the cash in bank left over will be divided equitably between all investors based on their account balances.

This payback method will continue until all debt is retired. Once the debt is retired, you are eligible to participate in profit sharing, as long as you remain in the network.

For example: After all the bills have been paid, let's say there is 100,000 cash left over. 40% would be $40,000. This would be divided among all the investors based on their investment percentages. If you have a 10% share, you would receive $4,000 for the quarter.

Dollar a Day Real Estate Investment Company

Promissory Note   Page 3

No Prepayment Penalty:

All or any part of the aforesaid principal sum and interest accrued may be prepaid at any time and from time to time without penalty.

Should Lender decide to sell Note, the Borrower shall have the first right of refusal to buy Lender 's interest.

Borrower has the right to substitute like collateral of equal or greater value.

Default

In the event of any default by the undersigned in the payment of principal or interest as stated in this contract or in the event of the suspension of actual business, (except due to the event of a natural disaster), insolvency, assignment for the benefit of creditors, adjudication of bankruptcy, or appointment of a receiver, of or against the undersigned, the unpaid balance of the principal sum of this promissory note shall at the option of the holder become immediately due and payable and the amount then due shall accrue interest until payment at the rate of five percent (5%) per annum.

Borrower and all other persons who may become liable for the payment hereof severally waive demand, presentment, protest, notice of dishonor or nonpayment, notice of protest, and any and all lack of diligence or delays in collection which may occur, and expressly consent and agree to each and any extension or postponement of time of payment hereof from time to time at or after maturity or other indulgence, and waive all notice thereof.

This note is made and executed under, and is in all respects governed by, the laws of the State of Florida.

Nancy Gaskins, DBA
Dollar-a-Day Real Estate Investment Company

Bio & Contact Info

Nancy Gaskins

Email: nancy.gaskins@operationHSH.com
Websites:www.iTrainInvestors.com, and www.nancygaskins.com

About Nancy

Nancy Gaskins radiates a super-charged, high-energy presence that immediately involves people and has them responding to her exciting challenge to desire, create, and live the American Dream! With her quick wit, flair for drama and unique insight into human behavior, Nancy delivers solid content and practical techniques that can be put to use immediately at work and home. For those who dare to leave a mediocre live behind, & desire to be extraordinary, just follow her sage advice!

Founder

Nancy Gaskins is the author of the "In Pursuit of the American Dream" life enrichment book series, Founder the *Armed Forces Real Estate Program*, (a Real Estate Agent Network, & Real Investment Program, and the *Dollar-a-Day Real Estate Investment Program.*

Background

Nancy's accomplishments & contributions have ranked her in the top 1% of all military spouses. She is a professional motivational speaker, author, and consultant specializing in Success & Achievement, Military Family

Life Issues, Real Estate Investing, Personal Finance, Entrepreneurship, and Leadership Development.

Nancy is a former Dean of Education, College Professor, Business Executive, & Entrepreneur. She has earned a Masters Degree in Business Administration (MBA) as well as a Bachelors Degree in Marketing. Nancy has completed additional post graduate level work, has previously held licenses in real estate, insurance, securities, and is considered a subject matter expert in a variety of business related fields.

Volunteer

Nancy is a proud US Army spouse that has 20+ years of experience with military families that span National Guard, Reserves, and Active Duty Army. She serves as an active volunteer and role model in her community serving in a variety of leadership positions, such as: FRG (Family Readiness Group) Leader, President of the ACS Private (Army Community Service) Organization, Vice-President of the Schweinfurt Community Spouses Club, AWAG (American Women's Activities in Germany) Speaker Chair, Franconian AWAG Conference Representative, AFAP (Army Family Action Plan) Delegate, AFTB Trainer (Army Family Team Building,) Member of the PWOC, (Protestant Women of the Chapel), and coaches children and parents on the benefits of Entrepreneurship and Financial Literacy.

Nancy is a 2008 Heroine of the Infantry, "Shield of Sparta," recipient, a distinction awarded from the National Infantry Association, and has earned the Presidential Volunteer Service Award in recognition of her volunteer work.

Family

Rob and Nancy just recently returned from a life-long dream of living in Europe, and are now enjoying the preparation for their upcoming retirement on the beautiful Emerald Coast of Florida. They have three wonderful grown children with families: Amanda & Chad, Rob Jr. & Nikki, Will & Shelley, and Jamie Hixson, a fabulous young lady the family "acquired" along the way. They are the proud grandparents of 8 grandchildren...Brayden, Danny, Bryce, Alex, Chad Jr., Will Jr., Kylee, and Kayla.

*** JOIN ME...Let's Connect! ***

Website: www.iTrainInvestors.com, and www.NancyGaskins.com

Facebook:
Nancy Sue Quinn-Gaskins

Publications:
Barnes and Noble Booksellers, (www.bn.com), Amazon, (www.Amazon.com,) & other online book retailers
Author Search: "Nancy Gaskins"

www.YouPublish.com/NancyGaskins

Twitter:
www.Twitter.com/NancyGaskins

Read my **BLOG**
http://nancygaskins.blogspot.com
Title of Blog: In Pursuit of the American Dream
Newspaper Articles/ other News: use the **Google** search engine:
"Nancy Gaskins," "Author Nancy Gaskins," "Dollar a Day Real Estate," "Live Like You Are Dying."

YouTube:
Search words: Dollar a Day Real Estate, Real Estate Investor, or Nancy Gaskins, Dollar a Day Real Estate investments, or Dollar a Day Real Estate Investor

Email: nancy.gaskins@operationHSH.com

Recommended Reading & Resources

Real Estate Investor Book Club & Resource Library

I am very much an advocate of training and development, trying to stay current on what is going on in the marketplace, and attempting to identify upcoming trends. Real Estate is evolving and we need to make sure that we all stay on top of our game.

I would like to know if any of you would be interested in participating in a real estate investor book club for the purpose of building a library and sharing resources with one another. My thoughts are that we would charge an annual fee of something like $25, and would use the membership fees to purchase all the top real estate investor training materials that are available in the marketplace. Books, DVDs, CD's, etcetera. We would poll our membership for recommendations of excellent resources, and of course, gladly accept donations.

We could host an online library website, where members could reserve a copy of whatever program or book they were interested in for the week or month. Whether to loan or charge a nominal fee for the rental would depend on the number of people willing to participate in the program and the actual expense of administering the program, including the library software program. Postage would be the only variable expense.

The whole point is to give everyone in the Dollar-a-Day Real Estate Investor Networks access to the best Real Estate investor training resources available in the industry... at an affordable price. I know we all are on tight budgets, so let's work together to figure out a way to make this happen!

Please let me know your thoughts by sending me an email ranking your top choices for topics that you are interested in learning more about:

- Foreclosures & Short Sales
- Rehabbing & Flipping properties

- No Money Down
- Options, Lease to Own, Subject to
- Tax Liens
- Property Management / Landlord duties
- Real Estate Math
- Commercial Real Estate Investing
- Residential Real Estate Investing
- Real Estate Agent Training
- Real Estate Investing (in general)
- Real Estate Investment Trusts (REITS)
- Other (please describe topic)

References for the American Dream

- Adams, James Truslow. (1931). *The Epic of America*. Simon Publications 2001 paperback: ISBN 1-931541-33-7

- Cullen, Jim. (2003). *The American Dream: A Short History of an Idea that Shaped a Nation*. Oxford University Press, 2004 paperback: ISBN 0-19-517325-2

- Fossum, Robert H., and John K. Roth. (1981). *The American Dream*. Edinburgh University Press. ISBN 0-9504601-6-8

- Luntz, Frank. "Americans Talk About the American Dream," in The New Promise of American Life, edited by Lamar Alexander and Chester E. Finn, Jr., Hudson Institute, Indianapolis (1995).

- Kochan, Thomas A. (2006). Restoring the American Dream: A Working Families' Agenda for America. The MIT Press. ISBN 0-262-61216-X.

- Samuelson, Robert J. (1995). *The Good Life and Its Discontents: The American Dream in the Age of Its Entitlement, 1945–1995*. New York: Vintage, 1997 paperback: ISBN 0-679-78152-8. Suggests raising the retirement age and means testing of entitlements to manage unfunded government commitments.

- Max Payne

What's Next?

It's YOUR company, remember? Send me your thoughts on products, services, and incentives that you would like to see the Dollar-a-Day Real Estate Investment Company offer to our network members.

BONUS

Challenge2Succeed
Master Plan for Life Management System

Strategic Planner Worksheets
Email to receive your FREE worksheets
Nancy.Gaskins@operationHSH.com

The Master Plan for Life Management System
7 Key Areas for a Well-balanced Life

Financial Fitness:
Income, Credit Score, Debt, Savings, Investments, Insurance, Assets, Overall Net Worth

Relationships:
Family (immediate & extended), Friends (local & long distance), Co-workers (bosses, colleagues, etc.),Neighbors

Health & Fitness:
Weight, Nutritional Habits, Medical care, Flexibility, Endurance, Balance, Strength, Exercise, Sports, etc.

R&R:
What you do for rest, relaxation, fun, recreation, & vacations

Self-Development:
Self-Improvement; anything you would like to learn, become, or do.

Contribution to Society:
Volunteer / Charity work; community, mentorships, spiritual, your legacy you wish to leave behind

Career / Home-maker:
Depending on your personal situation, your personal career aspirations, goals, education, & business relationships. Further subdivisions may be necessary. This also includes your career as a home-maker, military spouse, & American Patriot

PART VIII

Directory

Investor Directory
Preferred Real Estate Agents
Corporate Contributors
Sponsors

Invitation to Join:
To become a Dollar-a-Day Real Estate Investor, you must be referred by one of our registered Referral Partners and provide the Referral source on your Enrollment Application.

This Directory is updated on a quarterly basis, and the online version is updated on a continuous basis.

www.iTrainInvestors.com

Investor Network

Preferred Real Estate Agents

Sponsors

Corporate Contributors

Made in the USA
Lexington, KY
28 October 2013